"What better Lenten discipline and exercise than to ponder well, carefully, and daily our premier text on emancipation—the book of Exodus! Mary Alice Birdwhistell and Tyler D. Mayfield have written a study guide that is readily accessible for daily use. Surely Christians in Lent have no more important work to do than to engage the scriptural promises of and mandate to emancipation, especially in our world that is so bent on enslavement, the practice of cheap labor, and the systemic abuse of vulnerable lives. This book makes one wish that Lent were longer in order to do more of the Exodus. This is a most winsome invitation to fresh faith."

—Walter Brueggemann, William Marcellus McPheeters Professor Emeritus of Old Testament, Columbia Theological Seminary

"*Hard and Holy Work*, in its invitation to spiritual awakening and social action in the spirit of the liberator-prophet Moses, is pure gift in these days of global upheaval, inequity, and pain. The authors' writing is as compelling and brave as their vision of the church."

—Julie Pennington-Russell, Pastor, First Baptist Church of the City of Washington, DC

"*Hard and Holy Work* is an inspired guide for brave and curious Lenten travelers yearning for liberation. Be careful, though: Birdwhistell and Mayfield's intimate exploration of the Exodus saga refuses to skip past the perilous contradictions privileged readers are sure to encounter. Expect your journey inward with them to arrive at unexpected places."

—Amos J. Disasa, Senior Pastor, First Presbyterian Church of Dallas

"This inspiring guide illuminates the stories of Exodus alongside those of our time while inviting you to answer powerful questions and take bold, life-giving steps forward. It will encourage you to notice the holy ground you are living on and the holy experiences all around you while offering meaningful ways for you and your community to respond to injustice according to your context and situation. This is the guide for Lent that you have been waiting for."

—Angela Williams Gorrell, author of *The Gravity of Joy: A Story of Being Lost and Found*

"This lovely study and devotional is written with a wise and compassionate voice, bringing timely reflections on timeless Scriptures and nudging us to consider the significance of movements, moments, and our own spiritual yearnings. It is an invitation to pay attention, as the authors say, to 'the divine possibility of the present moment.' In a season in which our hearts are broken anew each day, may this book give us what we need as people of faith to mend and heal and move."

—Laura M. Cheifetz, coauthor of *Race in America: Christians Respond to the Crisis*

Hard and Holy Work

Hard and Holy Work

A Lenten Journey through the Book of Exodus

MARY ALICE BIRDWHISTELL
AND TYLER D. MAYFIELD

First Edition
Published by Westminster John Knox Press
Louisville, Kentucky

23 24 25 26 27 28 29 30 31 32—10 9 8 7 6 5 4 3 2 1

Scripture quotations from the book of Exodus are the translations of Tyler D. Mayfield. All other Scripture quotations are from the *New Revised Standard Version*, *Updated Edition*, copyright © 2021 National Council of Churches of Christ in the United States of America. Used by permission. All rights reserved worldwide.

Excerpt from Ron Bell, "Do Not Look Away," https://www.drronbell.com/post/do-not-look-away, May 29, 2020, reprinted by permission of the author. Excerpt from Kathryn Freeman, "Voices: Breonna Taylor, Invisible Black Women and God Who Sees Us," *Baptist Standard*, May 20, 2020, https://www.baptiststandard.com/opinion/voices/breonna-taylor-invisible-black-women-god-who-sees-us/, reprinted by permission of the author and the publisher. Excerpt from Mary Alice Birdwhistell and Lauren Jones Mayfield, "At Christmas, Jesus Bears the Light of Justice. We Need It More Than Ever," *Louisville Courier Journal*, December 18, 2020, reprinted by permission of the authors. Excerpt from Stephanie Kolin's prayer that begins "God Who Creates, God Who Redeems" is used by permission of the author.

All stories concerning other people are shared with permission.

Every effort has been made to determine whether texts are under copyright. If through an oversight any copyrighted material has been used without permission, and the publisher is notified of this, acknowledgment will be made in future printings.

Book design by Sharon Adams
Cover design by Allison Taylor

Library of Congress Cataloging-in-Publication Data is on file at the Library of Congress, Washington, DC.

ISBN-13: 978-0-664-26817-6

To the good people of Highland Baptist Church, who continually inspire and challenge us to join in the hard and holy work of God, creating a world where justice and love are abundant

Contents

Ash Wednesday: Beginning the Journey of Lent 1

The First Week of Lent: Not on My Watch 13
Exodus 1:8–2:10

The Second Week of Lent: Paying Attention, Seeing Injustice 27
Exodus 2:11–25

The Third Week of Lent: Look Again! 41
Exodus 3 and 4

The Fourth Week of Lent: Wade in the Water 59
Exodus 14

The Fifth Week of Lent: Finding God on Day 2 73
Exodus 16:2–30

Palm Sunday and Holy Week: The Next Right Thing 87
Exodus 17:1–7

Small-Group Study Guide 101

Acknowledgments 103

Notes 105

Ash Wednesday

Beginning the Journey of Lent

Sacred Geography of Louisville, Kentucky

In 1958 the Trappist monk Thomas Merton was visiting downtown Louisville when he had an unexpected spiritual revelation. Later he published a recounting of the event:

> In Louisville, at the corner of Fourth and Walnut, in the center of the shopping district, I was suddenly overwhelmed with the realization that I loved all those people, that they were mine and I theirs, that we could not be alien to one another even though we were total strangers . . . . There is no way of telling people that they are all walking around shining like the sun.[1]

It may seem odd for a monk, living a quiet and devoted life away from the hustle and bustle of the city, to come to a crowded street corner and have a spiritual awakening. However, Paul Pearson, director and archivist of Bellarmine University's Thomas Merton Center, notes that this pivotal moment "points to Merton's movement from being kind of an enclosed monk in the monastery, turning his back on the world, to beginning to turn toward the world." Pearson says, "[Merton] was cutting himself off from the world, but gradually he realizes you can't do that. That he's in the monastery for the world."[2] As he turned toward the challenges of the world, Merton would go on to champion justice issues and engage interfaith matters.

Walnut Street was a particularly fitting place for Merton's vision, given its predominance in the business life of African American Louisvillians during that time. As journalist Michael Washburn notes, "In 1958, years before the passage of both the Civil Rights Act and the Voting Rights Act, and only four years after the divisive *Brown v Board of Education* Supreme Court decision, Merton's feeling of human solidarity was experienced across race and economic lines in what was—and remains—a stubbornly stratified city."[3] Merton's place of epiphany later became a physical landmark in Louisville. Today, a plaque from the Kentucky Historical Society stands at the site of Merton's life-changing moment, and tourists from around the world visit this ordinary and extraordinary site. The corner of Fourth and Walnut stands as an invitation to pay attention, to truly see others, and to recognize the interconnected reality of our relationships. (By the way, if you ever search for the site, the city changed the name of Walnut Street to Muhammad Ali Boulevard in 1978 to honor another Louisvillian.)

Decades later, another site was created one block north and two blocks west of Merton's mystical experience. It became a memorial site for Breonna Taylor, the young Black medical worker who was shot and killed by Louisville police officers during a severely mishandled raid on her apartment in March 2020. Her murder, a significant event in our city and our country, contributed to the ever-growing national movement against police brutality and for racial justice. That summer, local protesters began gathering at Jefferson Square Park, a one-acre downtown park, and transformed it into what later became known as Injustice Square. They continued to gather here for the remainder of the year, building a community of resistance and accountability.

"They chose that park because, guess what, it's right in the middle of everything," Taylor's aunt Bianca Austin shared with the *Louisville Courier Journal*. "Injustice square is a statement for Breonna. That statement is that the injustice that y'all done to this woman, here it is, every day when you come to work, you need to be reminded of Breonna."[4] Today, Injustice Square Park remains the gathering space for local justice movements, protests, and gatherings. A new historical marker now stands alongside the park, at the corner of Sixth Street and Jefferson, calling us to take action against hatred, systemic evil, and forces of oppression.

These two sacred spaces—Fourth and Walnut and Injustice Square—encapsulate the two themes of this Lenten study: awakening and action. During this season of Lent, we invite you to consider these essential practices of spiritual life. There's something about Merton's invitation to pay attention at Fourth and Walnut that calls our feet to march toward the work of liberation at Injustice Square. And there's something about the work of justice and liberation that calls us toward a greater awakening to the world around us and to where God is within it. These two points on the city map are not in tension with one another but instead seem to be drawn toward one another. The pull between these two points in the sacred geography of Louisville reminds us that we cannot fully or faithfully live as the people God is calling and creating us to be without awakening *and* action.

Lent summons us in these exact directions. Traditionally Lent has been a season of pausing and self-reflection—an inward posture, but also, as part of that introspection, a time to engage in almsgiving—an outward posture. Paying attention and working for justice, then, deepen our Lenten practices and transform our understanding of them.

We (Tyler and Mary Alice) live and work in Louisville, and this place we call home significantly shapes our perspectives. Our church, Highland Baptist Church, is in the historic Highlands neighborhood of Louisville, just a couple miles from Merton's historical marker and Injustice Square. Highland is no stranger to this space between the contemplation of Merton's marker and the social action that arises from Injustice Square. In fact, the sacred space within Highland's stone walls has sparked a passion for various kinds of justice work in our community. The church has long championed the calling of women to ministry despite formerly being part of the Southern Baptist Convention, whose policy is that only men may serve as pastors. Highland has also become a space of radical welcome and affirmation of the LGBTQ+ community and has recently begun more intentional anti-racism and reparations work.

However, in the midst of this deep passion for justice within our church, Highland is also a predominantly white congregation with many resources in an affluent area of town. As a result, we often feel stuck, overwhelmed, or at a loss for how to best initiate and effect change in our city. We don't often know how to move from Merton's marker to Injustice Square, from awakening to action. And sometimes, in an effort not to go the *wrong* way, we end up not going any way at all.

As the writers of this study, we want to name from the beginning and seek vigilant awareness of the privilege and power we hold. We are both white, cisgender, heterosexual, well-educated professionals with stable jobs, and those identities come with advantages in our society. We are on a journey ourselves, and this book is an invitation: join us as we learn together about the work of justice. We do not pretend to have all the answers, and this study is not our attempt to fix all the complicated systems of injustice. Instead, it is our humble effort to take a faithful next step in the right direction. So we invite you to join us. We are traveling toward greater awareness of our world, with all its beauty and challenges, as the Spirit calls us toward justice and love.

Throughout this book, we will often write directly to others who occupy various spaces of privilege, but we hope that those who do not hold one or another form of privilege will also feel seen and cared for along the way. Privilege is not a yes-or-no proposition, a switch we flip one way or the other; we are all a combination of identities related to our gender, sexuality, economic level, educational background, race, ethnicity, and much more, and some of these identities provide us certain advantages. It's not about being right or wrong. As author Ijeoma Oluo notes, "Being privileged doesn't mean that you are always wrong and people without privilege are always right—it means that there is a good chance you are missing a few very important pieces of the puzzle."[5] This study asks us all to think deeply about those identities and how our society grants power and advantages to certain people simply because they belong to particular groups. The work of justice is to notice these systems and to work to correct them. This, too, is a part of the journey—and it will look different for each of us depending on how privilege intersects with our identities.

The idea for this book emerged from a sermon series based on the book of Exodus, which Mary Alice preached at Highland in the fall of 2020. Each week, as we reflected on the liberation of God's people in Exodus, the protests for justice for Breonna Taylor continued down the road from our church. Moved by the call to action that we were experiencing together, our pastors and congregation members joined in many of those protests, witnessing firsthand a long-overdue racial reckoning in our city and country. In those moments, we felt the synergy of reading the ancient wisdom of Exodus and responding to contemporary societal needs.

In addition, the protests and study of Exodus were taking place at the height of the COVID-19 pandemic, which exacerbated the extreme inequities among communities in resources, health care, education, access to medical supplies, technology, child care, and so much more. The pandemic brought the world as we had previously known it to a screeching halt and gave many of us an opportunity to reflect on our typical routines. Suddenly, we were paying attention in ways we never had before and asking ourselves, Where do we go from here? And how do we take brave steps forward in the ways that God is calling us?

These profound contexts—Merton's corner, Injustice Square, and our own privilege—shape our Lenten reflections as we focus on these two interconnected practices of spiritual life: awakening to the world around us and acting for liberation. Each of these dimensions enriches our lives of faith, and together they prepare us to be Easter people, people called to resurrection and new life. We welcome you to join us in this hard and holy work.

The Book of Exodus

During this Lenten season, we will explore selections from the biblical book of Exodus as one way to engage deeply in a life of reflection and action. Exodus is a book about an ancient people on a dramatic journey from enslavement in Egypt toward liberation. It concerns a liberating God who sees the oppression of God's people and acts to free them from bondage. Exodus tells the story of newly released Israelites. In addition, it serves as a model for people who find themselves searching for freedom in God's world. It speaks into Merton's life of contemplation and Injustice Square's demand for justice. Yet Exodus also tells of a people who wander in the wilderness with little idea of a next step. The book demonstrates the honest truth that the end of bondage does not always equate to immediate freedom. Thus, Exodus provides a paradigm for a contemporary, liberating spirituality.

Between the sacred geography of the world of the ancient Israelites and our contemporary world, Exodus has offered a way of liberation for Christian and Jewish communities through the ages. Many faithful people through the years have found their stories in these ancient stories. Exodus is a powerful story of faith and a popular resource for our theological imaginations.

In fact, the book's liberating message was perhaps feared as too inspiring by particular oppressors, such as enslavers, who attempted to quell the reading of these stories among their enslaved people. The "Slave Bible," as it was called, was created and published in 1807 by British missionaries specifically for use among enslaved Africans. The Slave Bible omitted various parts of Scripture, including, for example, Galatians 3:28, "There is no longer slave or free . . . for all of you are one in Christ Jesus," and the entire book of Revelation, which might offer too much hope about a new heaven and earth. The Slave Bible also left out Exodus 1–18, going straight from Genesis 45 (just before Jacob and his family go into Egypt to see Joseph) to Exodus 19 (when the Israelites arrive at Mount Sinai), omitting the entire story of the Israelites' escape from slavery under Pharaoh in the land of Egypt.[6] It is a significant reminder of how powerful these stories were (and still are) that they were considered too dangerous for enslaved people to access them. Even those who sought to oppose its message recognized the undeniable power of Exodus.

Yet the Exodus story still made its way into the hearts and souls of enslaved people, and over time it became compelling in more modern fights for freedom and justice as well. In a 2019 lecture titled "The Hope of Exodus in Black Theology," Andrew Prevot, a theology professor at Boston College, said that there came to be

> a tradition inaugurated by Black Christian slaves, who despite being subjected to coercive practices of non-education and mis-education, managed to discover another meaning of Christianity buried deep in the stories, images, and songs of their living faith. These resilient, material symbols of theological wisdom could

> not be made to communicate merely the politically crafted message of obedience to masters preached by apologists of American slavocracy. Something more was here: a mystery and a promise deeper than words: Christianity harbored a hope of Exodus. It whispered the dream of a divinely orchestrated escape from the death-dealing circumstances of the present order of things. It inspired a communal prayer for healing and freedom.[7]

In agreement with Prevot, we try to be intentional in the following pages by paying attention to marginalized voices in our modern world that bring new understanding and perspectives to the book of Exodus, perspectives perhaps never considered before. These voices lead us to assess our inherited interpretations, ponder more liberating readings, and experience anew the power of these stories for the work of liberation. Listening to the voices of marginalized communities becomes, then, a spiritual practice of awakening and ultimately action.

Today we read the biblical stories of the exodus in light of our own stories. The stories in the Bible should challenge, inspire, and beckon us to pay attention to what is happening in the world around us. How do these stories remind us of who we are as the people of God wandering through the wilderness of this moment, seeking to find our way to liberation and freedom? How do these stories speak to people of privilege, calling us to see injustice and to act against it? These are just a few questions to consider as we engage the hard and holy work of this season.

How to Use This Book during Lent

Lent provides us with a focused opportunity to explore the much-needed connection between spiritual awakening and social action. Each chapter of this book coincides with a week of the Lenten journey and with a story from the book of Exodus. You are invited to read the chapter at any point during the week. You might read the chapters in anticipation of meeting with a group to discuss it, or you may use this book as an individual study. We are mindful that this faithful work is difficult, and we aren't meant to do it alone. If feasible and suitable, find a way to take this journey with others.

At the conclusion of each chapter, we invite you to reflect, engage, and respond to what you have read. Each week, there are activities you can do individually or with a group that invite you to develop a more profound sense of awareness and then to find ways to respond to that awareness in the world around you. All three sections—Paying Attention, Sharing Together, and Taking Action—are crucial to this Lenten study; they are not afterthoughts. Not all the suggested questions and activities may suit your context and lived reality. We have attempted to provide a plethora of options for a variety of situations. If you find that a question or activity does not speak to you, we hope you will skip it without worry or guilt. Move freely and use options from different categories throughout the week, practicing attention and exploring ways to take action each day.

These chapter conclusions are not quizzes with right and wrong answers; they are invitations to continue to ponder how this Lenten season and the book of Exodus speak into your life today. These activities may not be ones you have engaged in before. We hope they will be transformative in ways that extend beyond the Lenten season.

Paying Attention will ask you to be present to God, to Scripture, to the world around you, and to yourself. We invite you to be still, get curious, ask questions, and allow yourself to be uncomfortable in these moments of wondering, curiosity, and contemplation. These practices will be offered as daily exercises for mostly individual use.

Sharing Together will provide questions for you to engage in this week's reading with a small group, colleague, or friend. Free videos for each session of the study are also available at https://tinyurl.com/WJKYouTube. These short videos of us introducing each chapter can help provide you with a starting point to engage with and discuss the book each week. You can use them to begin group sessions or as an introduction for each participant to watch beforehand.

Taking Action will give concrete opportunities for you to engage in your community in hands-on ways. This work is not merely intellectual or spiritually inward; we hope this

Lenten season engages you in the outward work of justice and liberation.

The Cry of Ash Wednesday

It may feel peculiar to start the spiritual journey of Lent with a day dedicated to dust. It is sobering to sit in pews in the middle of a week and hear the words, "Remember you are dust, and to dust you will return." It may be uncomfortable to feel the grit and grime of ashes on our forehead and to reflect on our mortality. As pastors, it feels gut-wrenching to look into the eyes of loved ones while reminding them of this harsh reality. Ash Wednesday takes our breath away and invites us to lean into the vulnerability of these uncomfortable moments. I (Tyler) will never forget the Ash Wednesday service when I sat in the pews and watched my wife, a minister, impose ashes first on an elderly gentleman dying of cancer and then on the forehead of our eight-year-old son. What a poignant reminder of our finitude.

Ash Wednesday also cries out for us to pay attention! This day reminds us that, despite believing and even living as if we are immortal, we are, in fact, human, each one of us. Ash Wednesday smacks us in the middle of the forehead with the realization that the life entrusted to us is precious and fragile. For some of us, it wakes us from the privilege and comfort of our day-to-day lives. For others, it reminds us, all too well, of the ever-present brokenness of the world and the frailty of life that we experience every day. For all of us, Ash Wednesday challenges us to sit in the discomfort of these hard and holy truths and pushes us into the wilderness of Lent.

Author Anne Lamott reminds us, "Faith includes noticing the mess, the emptiness and discomfort, and letting it be there until some light returns."[8] And so, this Lent, we invite you to join us in what may be an unsettling spiritual journey. After all, if we continually linger in spaces of comfort, familiarity, and certainty, do we ever really change? Do we ever really grow? So much of our lives is about seeking comfort and convenience. Yet perhaps the journey of faith, if it is going to stretch us or move us beyond our expectations and imaginations, is going to be a difficult one that causes us to be unsettled.

What a hard and holy invitation! But it is also an invitation we hope will lead to transformation within us and our world.

As we begin the Lenten journey together, may we remember to be present to the sacred geography of this moment. May we turn aside and pay attention to the burning bushes in our wilderness, in unexpected people and unlikely places. As Cole Arthur Riley notes, "Contemplative spirituality is a fidelity to beholding the divine in all things. In the field, on the walk home, sitting under the oak tree that hugs my house. A sacred attention."[9] May we listen to the voices and circumstances calling us to join in this hard and holy work.

Lenten Practices

Paying Attention

(Self-Reflection)

Wednesday

As we begin the Lenten journey today, take a moment to welcome your experiences throughout this journey—thoughts, feelings, situations, or emotions that may make you joyful or uncomfortable. Offer a prayer of openness to this season and God's presence with you during this time of reflection and action.

Thursday

Have you ever experienced a moment of epiphany or spiritual realization in which you discovered or sensed a new direction or insight? It does not need to be as dramatic as Merton's to be meaningful. Perhaps you saw with fresh perception something you had seen many times before. Or maybe you saw something for the first time. How did that epiphany moment change you?

Friday

What has been your previous experience of noticing injustice as a vital part of your spiritual practice? Are you accustomed to discerning justice as a part of the life of faith? Have you considered working against injustice as a spiritual discipline?

Saturday

Consider the sacred geography of your life that calls you to pay attention and act for justice. What is your corner of Walnut and Fourth? What is your Injustice Square? Maybe you can think of smaller places and moments where injustices occur that aren't marked in such public ways.

Sharing Together
(Group Discussion Questions)

1. What are some of the points of the sacred geography of your own life that have shaped who you are today? What markers in your life journey and identity affect what you bring to this space together?
2. What knowledge of the book of Exodus do you bring to this study? Do you remember particular stories about Moses or the Israelites?
3. How does the existence of the Slave Bible make you feel? What might be so powerful about some of these biblical stories that led enslavers to censor them?
4. How do you understand the book's title phrase, "hard and holy work"? Can you think of an example from your own spiritual life that has been both hard and holy?

Taking Action
(Next Steps)

1. Make a concrete plan for ways that you will carve out space to engage this study and respond. For example, you may need a daily or weekly schedule to complete the readings. Perhaps you need to invite a friend or group to join you. How will you observe a holy Lent in our rushed and busy world?
2. Take time to notice injustices in the news, on social media, in the world around you. Instead of walking away from the discomfort, lean into it. Pray for those experiencing such injustice. What does this stir in you?

3. Research the sacred geography of your own community. What points have been the spaces for spiritual awakening or social action? Is there any connection between them? Visit these spaces, or learn what you can about them online.

4. Share with friends—in person or on social media—your broad hopes for this Lenten journey.

Not on My Watch

Exodus 1:8–2:10

Maybe Love and Attention Are the Same Thing

There's an illuminating scene in the movie *Lady Bird* when high school senior Christine McPherson (played by Saoirse Ronan) meets with one of the nuns at her Catholic school to discuss her college entrance essay, which is about growing up in Sacramento. Christine cannot wait to get out of Sacramento, which seems so dull and lifeless to her, and she is applying to colleges across the country in search of a place where her life can feel more significant. After reading her essay, Sister Sarah-Joan (played by Lois Smith) says, "You clearly love Sacramento." And Christine replies, "I do?"

The nun says, "Well, you write about Sacramento so affectionately, and with such care."

"I was just describing it," Christine says, brushing it off.

"It comes across as love," Sister Sarah-Joan insists.

Christine finally admits, "Sure, I guess I pay attention [to things here]."

The nun's response seems to be as much for those watching the movie as it is for the strong-willed eighteen-year-old in her office. She says, "Don't you think maybe they are the same thing? Love and attention?" Ultimately, one of the ironies of the movie is that not until Christine goes off to college in New York does she realize just how much she loves Sacramento after all.[1]

The nun may be correct; love and paying attention might be the same thing. I (Tyler) remember my first few months as a new parent; I paid attention to every little coo, every grin, every cry, and every new sound my infant daughter made. Or think about the first days after moving into a house or apartment and how you suddenly begin to pay attention to all the unique features of your new home. I (Mary Alice) had never paid such close attention to paint colors, window shades, or light fixtures until I moved into my first house. Suddenly, all of these things became important to me. I was paying attention!

Paying attention with care and concern is a crucial marker of our spiritual lives as well. In fact, it is an important spiritual discipline; and no one can do this hard and holy work for us.

Our Lenten journey continues this week at the beginning of the exodus story with a reminder that we follow a God who sees us—a God who is also paying attention. Before the Hebrew people are rescued from slavery, before Moses arrives at the burning bush or the Red Sea waters part, they first meet a God who sees them in their distress.

This week we consider the theme of a God who sees—and not merely sees but also pays deep attention. How might we attend, as God does, to those often ignored, and then act on our new vision?

Women Conspiring against Pharaoh

If you are a fan of *The Handmaid's Tale,* either the book by Margaret Atwood or the television series on Hulu, you know that in the Republic of Gilead, women are stripped of their rights and placed into different categories within this fictional society. Each woman wears a color based on her specific role. For instance, the commanders' wives wear only shades of blue. The Marthas, the household servants, wear green. The young girls wear pink. And the Handmaids, assigned to each commander, are known for their signature red dress and white hat.

The Handmaid's Tale is gut-wrenching to watch because of how women are treated and how they inflict their pain on one another. However, a glimmer of hope arises in season 3, when a group of women—Handmaids, Marthas, and even commanders' wives—begin conspiring together against the men ruling over them. As the main character June says, "They never should have given us uniforms if they didn't want us to become an army."

When we read the opening two chapters of Exodus, we are reminded of *The Handmaid's Tale* in the ways we see powerful women conspiring against Pharaoh, the king of Egypt, who represents the traditional power structure.

In Exodus 1:8–9, Pharaoh is worried about the increasing number of Israelites: "There are more Hebrews than there are Egyptians, and they're getting stronger than we are. We must do something about this situation." But his plan to oppress the Israelites and force them into laboring for him does not fare well; instead, the Israelites continue to increase in number under the excruciating service to the Egyptians. God's people multiply. Feeling threatened and powerless, Pharaoh devises a nefarious plan and tells two Hebrew midwives—Shiphrah and Puah—to kill any Hebrew baby boys who are born but allow the baby girls to live. It is clear Pharaoh does not consider women or girls to be a threat to his power or empire. But baby boys are another story!

Pharaoh is incredibly mistaken. These women, Shiphrah and Puah (who are surprisingly given names in a text that often leaves marginalized people nameless), do not listen to this unnamed pharaoh or follow his demands:

> But the midwives feared God; they did not do as the king of Egypt told them. But they let the children live. (v. 17)

Shiphrah and Puah strategically play to Pharaoh's bias toward Hebrew women and their fertility, saying, "It's the most amazing thing, Pharaoh, but the Hebrew women are nothing like the refined Egyptian women you are accustomed to. Hebrew women are like animals. They deliver so quickly, and the baby just plops right out of them before we can even get there to help." And it seems that Pharaoh believes them.

Shiphrah and Puah have become some of our biblical heroes for how they cleverly and courageously stand up to Pharaoh. As writer Nadia Bolz-Weber said, "Sometimes, the most holy thing we can say is, 'No—not on my watch.'"[2] These truly vulnerable women refuse to follow the king's villainous scheme and use his fears against him. They realize the absurdity of his lethal request and choose, boldly and faithfully, not to obey the most powerful person in the kingdom. They resist.

When Pharaoh realizes his plan has not worked, he orders that any Hebrew baby boy born must be thrown into the Nile River (v. 22). If not killed at birth, they would be killed in their infancy. Pharaoh is obsessed with the destruction of those he sees as inferior. He is a man of death, and he has doubled down on his threat.

Not long after this cruel command, a Hebrew woman, Jochebed, gives birth to a son (2:2). But like Shiphrah and Puah, she also says to Pharaoh's order, "No—not on my watch." She hides her baby at home for three months to protect him from the deadly fate of the Nile, until she realizes that she cannot keep him a secret much longer. Can you imagine this stressful time for the mother and her newborn? How do you keep a newborn quiet? The pharaoh of Egypt wants her son, her "fine baby" (v. 2), dead. So, in an attempt to save his life, she places her baby in a basket and sends him floating down the Nile River (v. 3). Some might ask, What kind of mother would ever place her baby in a basket or send him into such a dangerous situation? It is a risky decision indeed, but we might reflect today on parents who take their children across the border of their country and into the United States. The only motivation is for her child to survive; this mother is willing to do whatever it takes to save her child's life.

Did Moses' mother have a plan? Some biblical scholars wonder if she knows *where* she is sending the basket—if she knows it will likely float right past Pharaoh's palace, located farther down the river. If she knows this, it makes her actions here even riskier. For her baby to survive, the right person must find him.

Which is precisely what happens. Pharaoh's daughter is bathing in the river and comes upon the baby in the basket. She knows immediately that the infant must be one of the Hebrew children her father has commanded to be killed.

> The daughter of Pharaoh came down to bathe along the river, while her female attendants walked beside the river. She saw the papyrus basket among the reeds and sent her slave to bring it. She opened it and saw the child. The boy was crying! She

> had compassion upon him and said, "This one must be from the children of the Hebrews." (vv. 5–6)

She, too, says, "No—not on my watch," and begins to wonder what she might do to save this child's life. Unlike her father, she shows compassion for the Hebrew baby, disregarding her father's command.

Meanwhile, another courageous woman is watching this rescue scene unfold. Moses' big sister—we will later learn her name, Miriam—has been following the basket down the river. When she sees Pharaoh's daughter find him, she must be giddy with excitement. She immediately approaches Pharaoh's daughter, saying, "Is that a baby in that basket?! Oh my goodness. How awful! How can I help? What if I could find a Hebrew woman to nurse this child for you? I might know someone who might be willing to do that." Pharaoh's daughter responds, "Oh yes, absolutely. Great idea! I'll send wages to the woman who watches after this baby and keeps him safe." So, in the end, Moses' own mother is paid by the princess to watch over her own baby, on Pharaoh's dime no less. The child whom Pharaoh wanted to drown in the Nile is saved from that same river by Pharaoh's daughter, abetted by a loving mother and a watchful sister.

These women undermine Pharaoh's power cleverly and intentionally to bring a new life into the world. Whereas the mighty Pharaoh is fixated on death, violence, and annihilation, the women harbor life. He commands; they resist. These women pay attention to the injustice surrounding them and take action.

Womanist biblical scholar Wil Gafney points out that the two midwives, Shiphrah and Puah, "become the first deliverers in the book of deliverance."[3] They point us to who God is: A God who is interested in life. A God who delivers us. A God who takes risks on us. A God who wades into the water to come to us. A God who takes notice of us, who is aware and awake. A God who says, "No—not on my watch."

The hope of the exodus story begins to come to life through these women who notice God's people suffering in the land of Egypt. Because we have a God who *sees* us. Even when we humans don't pay attention, God sees and teaches us to do the same.

The God Who Sees (Gen. 16)

> So she named the Lord who spoke to her, "You are El-roi," for she said, "Have I really seen God and remained alive after seeing him?" (Gen. 16:13)

The women in Moses' story remind us of another biblical woman whom God sees—Hagar. In Genesis 16, Hagar, a girl given to Sarai as a slave, is oppressed by Sarai. Why? Because after Sarai suggests that her husband Abram sleep with Hagar, Hagar conceives. Sarai becomes jealous and angry. The story uses the same Hebrew word for Sarai's actions toward Hagar as Exodus 1:11 uses for the Egyptians' oppression of the Israelites. It is not mild mistreatment but cruelty and abuse.

The plight of Hagar, also an Egyptian, allows us to draw multiple connections between the two stories. When Hagar runs to the wilderness to escape Sarai, God's messenger finds her and offers a blessing concerning her soon-to-be-born son, Ishmael. The divine blessing she receives in Genesis 16:10 sounds like the one God gave to Abram earlier in Genesis: "I will so greatly multiply your offspring that they cannot be counted for multitude." In response to this angelic appearance and blessing, Hagar names God *El-roi,* "The God Who Sees." This enslaved Egyptian girl becomes the first person in the Bible to give God a name, a name based on her experience of being seen by God. It is the first attribute of God that is recognized by a human and used as a name—the Seeing God.

God indeed sees the injustice and abandonment of Hagar. God sees the inhospitable place to which she has run, and God responds with a blessing.

We All Want to Be Seen

Isn't that what we want—to be seen? This text, and these women, beckon us toward the God who sees us—no matter where we find ourselves.

If you have played hide-and-seek with small children, you have seen an illustration of wanting to be seen. Although they want to hide and love the suspense of the game, they also want to be found. It can be difficult for them to remain hidden and unfound. I (Tyler) remember clearly how my kids' desire to be seen by a loved one was often greater than their wish to conceal themselves, resulting in noisy hints and even jumping out of their hiding places prematurely. Sometimes all I had to do was walk into the room where they were hiding and ask playfully, "Where are you?" for them to reveal themselves happily. We all want connection with one another.

I (Tyler) also remember visiting for the first time an elderly homebound member of my church. He greeted me at the door in his wheelchair and instructed me to sit down. He then began to talk and share stories out of his profound loneliness, hoping I might see him and honor his life. He fought in World War II long before my parents' births, and his memories of that time were still vivid and compelling. So I sat, listened, and tried to be affirming of his memories as we reminisced for a while. I hoped to communicate in that sacred moment in his living room that I saw him as a companion on the journey, valued his life, and honored his memories. Paying attention to his stories was my small way of showing concern for him and appreciating his experiences.

I (Mary Alice) remember the day a grandmother called our church office and asked if Highland would be a safe space to bring her teenaged grandchild, Hazel, who identified as transgender. We have many LGBTQ+ members of our youth community and welcomed this new family to join us. When I (Mary Alice) first met Hazel, they often kept their face down and their head covered, almost as if to keep themself hidden—because they still didn't know for sure if this was a space where they could be fully themself. But over time, I watched as Hazel stood up a little taller, a little more confident, until finally, when my colleague Justin and I met with them to talk about baptism, we saw Hazel's radiant smile, their face glowing with excitement about what they had experienced. On Hazel's baptism day, the congregation watched in awe as Hazel came up out of the waters, their face beaming with pure joy. During the congregational response, Hazel slowly looked to each person around the room that day as if to savor the gift of being seen exactly as they are, a beloved child of God.

Actress Jodie Foster gave an incredibly moving speech at the 2013 Golden Globe Awards, where she received the Lifetime Achievement

Award. The audience was mesmerized by her boldness and vulnerability as she shared details about her life, her sexuality, and her family. At the end, she shared the following words:

> This feels like the end of one era and the beginning of something else. . . . And maybe it won't be as sparkly, maybe it won't open on 3,000 screens, maybe it will be so quiet and delicate that only dogs can hear it whistle. But it will be my writing on the wall. Jodie Foster was here, I still am, and I want to be seen, to be understood deeply and to be not so very lonely.[4]

Here was an exceptionally talented Hollywood star, receiving a Lifetime Achievement Award at the Golden Globes, who had been on every television and movie screen in America, yet, at the end of the day, all she wanted was to be seen and understood. Perhaps if we are willing to be as honest and vulnerable as Jodie Foster, in different ways, that is what we want too.

But Are We All Seen?

How many in our society do not feel seen or supported? How many living in marginalized communities have been made to feel entirely invisible? If we listen to the voices of those not in power, we begin to grasp a harsh reality: so many people feel unseen. They are not taken seriously because of their gender, race, sexuality, nationality, or other factors. Our culture routinely sidelines them. For example, many astute observers noted how her death was met with silence in the days after Breonna Taylor was murdered, especially when compared to #IRunwithAhmaud, which went viral after the murder of twenty-five-year-old Ahmaud Arbery.

Kathryn Freeman wrote a powerful article after the murder of Breonna Taylor about "the cloak of invisibility [that] envelops the suffering of Black women."[5] Freeman writes,

> There is a notable difference in how the deaths of Black women are met by our culture . . . .

> The irony of the lack of the attention to state violence against Black women is that for centuries black women—like Sojourner Truth, Ida B. Wells, Mamie Till, Rosa Parks, Jo Ann Robinson, Alicia Garza, Patrisse Cullors and Opal Tometi—have done and are doing the unseen work of organizing, documenting and protesting white supremacy and misogyny in this country.
>
> Black women, out of a deep sense of love and desire for freedom for themselves and for others, are committed to this often backbreaking and soul-crushing work, perhaps reasoning if we can free ourselves, then we can free our Black brothers and non-Black sisters from chains of racism and misogyny that for so long have gripped this nation and our church.

We, as the authors of this study, want to name the many ways in which we, too, have failed or refused to see, to awaken and pay attention to, the suffering of many marginalized people and communities around us. We are complicit in ignoring the pain. We are accustomed to not focusing our attention on these overlooked communities.

I (Mary Alice) certainly have a deep awareness of sexism as a woman, particularly as a pastor in a denomination dominated by men. Likewise, as someone who has a bone disorder called osteogenesis-imperfecta, I can't not see how society excludes those of us with disabilities. However, as a white, educated, cisgender, straight woman, I lived much of my life with little awareness of racism, homophobia, and transphobia. It wasn't until my late twenties, through a relationship with a Black man, that I slowly began to see the world through his eyes in ways that would change me forever. Even then, I acknowledge that this was just the tip of the iceberg. I'm still very much on a journey of learning to dig more deeply to see the pain and trauma that is buried so deeply beneath the water.

Likewise, I (Tyler) hold substantial privilege due to my race, gender, sexual orientation, class, physical ability, and religion. All the advantages of this social location are only becoming clearer to me as I encounter people with differing life experiences. For example, my wife and I are both ordained clergy, but she is the only one who receives inappropriate comments from congregants about her attire on Sunday mornings. Another example: after I had served on the faculty at my first teaching job for about a year, my wife became pregnant with our third child. I thought nothing about writing to my colleagues to share the good news. One of my fellow faculty members and dear friends shared with me that as a lesbian she would have thought twice about sharing such news so publicly and spontaneously. What felt perfectly natural to me as someone in a heterosexual relationship felt sensitive to her. She knew that no one would question my wife's pregnancy because it's considered ordinary for a married heterosexual couple to have children. People—even progressive academics—would have questions about the private matters of her life if she made the same announcement. She would likely have to navigate intimate inquiries. Today, looking back on my spontaneous announcement, I consider also the challenges that some heterosexual couples have with fertility. My email to colleagues was meant as an expression of joy—and it was likely received by my colleagues as such—but it also demonstrated how I benefited from my identities as married and heterosexual.

Those who regularly feel seen and heard often do not truly recognize the frustration and pain of marginalized communities. We know how much it matters to feel seen, and we know that systems are at work to ensure entire people groups remain invisible. For example, systemic racism is found in the discriminatory rules and regulations of nearly every area of modern life, including the criminal justice system, employment, health care, housing, and education. One brief example of racial discrimination within our education system involves school discipline. The American Psychological Association's publication *Monitor on Psychology* noted in 2016, "According to 2013–14 data collected by the U.S. Department of Education's Office of Civil Rights, black K–12 students are 3.8 times as likely as their white peers to receive one or more out-of-school suspensions."[6] Further studies have shown that this difference is not because Black students are creating more problems than white students. Another example involves the criminal justice system in America: although Black people represent 14 percent of the population (in 2019), they make up 33 percent of the total prison population.[7] This racial disparity is a tragic feature of our prison system that can be traced to numerous discriminatory practices. Several related systems work together to marginalize and make these people groups invisible.

It is both tragic and unacceptable that those whose identities are sidelined go unseen.

I Know God Watches Me

To a people who have felt invisible and unseen, God reminds the people of Israel throughout the book of Exodus that God sees them. How interesting that here in the very beginning of Exodus, the people who mirror the way God will take action later in the book are *all* women: Shiphrah, Puah, Moses' mother and sister Miriam, and Pharaoh's daughter—all described as people who "see"—who are paying attention to the world around them and who are ready to respond at a moment's notice.

In 1905, the songwriter Civilla Martin was visiting a friend, Mrs. Doolittle, whose poor health had left her bedridden for twenty years. When Civilla's husband asked Mrs. Doolittle how she managed to have hope amid such difficulty, she referred to Jesus' words from the Gospel of Matthew, "Are not two sparrows sold for a penny? Yet not one of them will fall to the ground apart from your Father . . . . So do not be afraid; you are of more value than many sparrows." In her own words, Mrs. Doolittle's response to the question was simple, "His eye is on the sparrow, and I know He watches me."[8] From that encounter, Civilla went on to write this song:

> Why should I feel discouraged?
> Why should the shadows come?
> Why should my heart be lonely
> and long for heaven and home,
> when Jesus is my portion?
> My constant friend is he:
> his eye is on the sparrow,
> and I know he watches me.

> I sing because I'm happy,
> I sing because I'm free,
> for his eye is on the sparrow,
> and I know he watches me.[9]

Years later, the song became a popular Black gospel song, sung by Ethel Waters and then by Mahalia Jackson, whose singing of it became an essential part of the soundtrack to the Civil Rights Movement.

God is watching over you. God sees you. And when God sees oppression and suffering, God says, "No—not on my watch." Like Shiphrah and Puah, like Moses' mother and sister, like Pharaoh's daughter, and like the people we will discover throughout Exodus, our God is raising up deliverers among us. As biblical scholar Wil Gafney reminds us, "Sometimes some of us look more like the Egyptians doing the oppressing and sometimes some of us look more like the Israelites being oppressed. And God is watching all of us, listening for the cry of the broken-hearted, raising up deliverers from among us to do the work of justice."[10]

As we begin to reflect and see more deeply this Lent, we must follow the example of a God who sees. Those of us who have the privilege of being seen must work to correct our habits of ignoring and not seeing, and to awaken to how the overabundance of attention we receive affects those who go unseen. As Nigerian American author Ijeoma Oluo states, "When we identify where our privilege intersects with somebody else's oppression, we'll find our opportunities to make real change."[11] We must follow the example of a God who sees—and then moves.

Lenten Practices

Paying Attention

(Self-Reflection)

Monday

How might you discern situations in this first week of Lent in which God is calling you to say, "No—not on my watch"? Consider this short prayer of discernment to use throughout your day: "Help me, O God, to see anew what is mine to do."

Tuesday

How are you beginning to sense that God might be calling you to become courageous and ingenious like Shiphrah and Puah? What acts of courageous risk-taking is God calling you to live out?

Wednesday

How aware are you of the injustices happening in your neighborhood? Who might you connect with today to learn more about those injustices?

Thursday

How do you discern situations in which God is calling you to respond? Try this prayer again today: "Help me, O God, to see anew what is mine to do."

Friday

Consider areas of life and situations where women are not equally represented as leaders: politics, the church, business, and so on. Look up the statistics of women's representation in various areas of life and work around you. Reflect on what this data means in the world today.

Saturday

Draw a picture expressing the idea of a God who sees. Look around your environment for inspiration, using whatever tools are available, and trust that it's good enough. If you wish, share your art with others. Ask what they see in your work.

Sharing Together

(Group Discussion Questions)

1. Name and reflect on a time when you personally felt seen by God.
2. Tell about a time when you did not feel seen or heard by the people around you. What would have helped to make you feel visible?

3. Who (individually or as a group) is not being seen today—in your religious community, neighborhood, city, or the world?
4. Can you think of times when you realize you haven't truly "seen" someone?

Taking Action
(Next Steps)

1. Practice being aware in a new way this first week of Lent. As you go about your days, pause to truly notice people and situations. Take the time to genuinely ask how someone—a friend or perhaps a person you see regularly but don't interact with—is doing, and listen deeply.
2. What else can you do this week to make someone feel your care? Write a note. Bake a treat to share. Take time for a personal visit or phone call. Make a donation in honor or memory of someone special.
3. If you want to learn more about race, including topics such as privilege, intersectionality, affirmative action, and cultural appropriation, we recommend Ijeoma Oluo's book *So You Want to Talk About Race.*

Paying Attention, Seeing Injustice

Exodus 2:11–25

Missing the Chicken

The classic jump rope game Double Dutch requires significant spatial awareness as players determine just the right moment to jump over the ropes that are being rotated around them at various speeds. In 2014, *National Geographic* asked participants in a study to watch a video of people wearing green, yellow, red, and purple T-shirts who were jumping rope and to count the number of times the green team members jumped over the rope. These were experienced jump ropers, and participants would need to watch the video closely to count the correct number of jumps. Forty percent of test participants gave the correct answer: thirty-eight jumps.

They were then asked if they noticed anything else during the Double Dutch game—because, in the midst of the thirty-eight jumps, a person dressed in a chicken costume walked into the middle of the camera frame, did a "funky chicken dance," and walked off stage. Very few people noticed the chicken at all, even though they had been staring right at it! Also, during the thirty-second video the color of the wall behind the jumpers slowly changed from bright blue to bright red, and almost everyone missed this significant change on the screen in front of them.[1]

Psychology researcher Daniel Simons conducted a similar experiment in 1999. Viewers watched a video intently to count the number of times a ball was exchanged between one person and another. The results were the same no matter where the video was shown: nearly half of the people who took the test completely missed the person who came into the picture in an animal suit. In fact, when these participants were told about the animal, many protested that the experiment had to have been rigged. They argued they must have been shown two different videos, because there's no way they could have missed something so obvious when they had been staring right at the screen.

In response to the experiment, Simons explains that "We consciously see only a small subset of our visual world, and when our attention is focused on one thing, we fail to notice other, unexpected things around us—including those we might want to see."[2]

As we continue to make our Lenten journey through Exodus, we focus on Moses' ability to pay attention to the injustices around him. We consider our own obstacles to seeing and how Lent invites us to wake up to these failures of attention. We contemplate what prevents us from paying attention. Where are we missing the chicken in the story?

Moses Pays Attention

> And it came to pass when Moses was older, he went out to his siblings, and he saw the burden of their forced labor. (Exod. 2:11)

Last week we explored the early life of Moses as he is placed precariously into the river in an attempt to save his life. He is found by Pharaoh's daughter, who ends up paying Moses' mother to nurse him. He is saved and temporarily restored to his family. The story concludes in Exodus 2:10 by noting that Moses' mother brings him back to be raised by Pharaoh's daughter. Moses grows up in Pharaoh's palace with the Egyptians, all the while knowing his people are Hebrew and not Egyptian. The story omits the details of his childhood and any internal struggle he might have felt being Hebrew while living in an Egyptian household.

At the beginning of the next scene, in Exodus 2:11, Moses is watching his people, the Hebrews, work. He is overcome by the reality that all of them are enslaved, working as forced laborers. Exodus 1:8–11 notes that the Egyptians oppressed the Hebrews in order to control their population and power. As Moses is paying attention to this unjust exploitation, he sees an Egyptian beating a Hebrew person. Unable to stand by idly, Moses saves the Hebrew, killing the Egyptian and hiding his body in the sand (2:12).

We might read about this brief and deadly encounter and think, Well, it's great that he saved his brother, the Hebrew, but did he have to kill the Egyptian? Was that necessary? This is a crucial question when we encounter violence of any type in biblical stories. We may be tempted to skip over such violent incidents or ignore them entirely because we honor Moses as a great hero, one who becomes aware of his people's suffering and ultimately acts to help liberate them. But we need to pause and linger over this brutal event, not to justify the action but at least to contextualize it within the world of the exodus story. We take this violence seriously by thinking deeply about its use here in the narrative and within the wider world.

Old Testament scholar Terence Fretheim says it's important theologically to note how many of Moses' actions in Exodus parallel God's actions later in the story.[3] For instance, Moses sees Israel's oppression in Exodus 2:11, just as God sees it in 2:25. Likewise, the same verb that is used to describe Moses striking the Egyptian in verse 12 is also used to describe God's actions toward the Egyptians in 3:20 and 12:12–13, when God strikes Egypt with different plagues. Fretheim argues that using the same verb ("strike") would not have been considered inappropriate by the narrator because it anticipates God's subsequent actions. It foreshadows God's more active resistance toward injustice in the coming chapters. Both God and Moses move from seeing to action.

These literary observations, of course, do not ultimately validate the violence in this passage, and we still need to sit with the discomfort of violence on a human level. It is important to ask whether violence is ever an appropriate form of resistance to injustice. However, it is also important to note that our understanding of the use of violence may be culturally different from that of the ancient storytellers. The emphasis in this story seems to focus on Moses' relationship with his "brothers" and his attention to their suffering. Some readers may see Moses' actions as a failure of leadership, and we would, of course, want to condemn homicide in the strongest terms; yet for the purposes of this study, we want to draw attention to Moses' ability to see the injustice around him. His subsequent actions may not have been constructive, but his attention to exploitation is worthy of our attention.

> When Moses went out the next day, he was surprised to see two Hebrew people fighting. (2:13)

The next day, Moses again "sees" as God does, when Moses observes two Hebrews fighting. This time the enmity stems not from the Egyptians' oppression but from infighting between the Hebrews. Again, something does not seem right, and Moses is paying attention. Moses intervenes to address the injustice, confronting the person in the wrong, just as God will confront Pharaoh through Moses in the days ahead.

After he learns that his violent deed is known, Moses flees to the land of Midian, where he sees shepherds driving women away from a well as they are drawing water for their father's flock (vv. 15–17). Once again, something isn't right about this scene, and Moses is paying attention. He rushes to their rescue, and the same verb used when Moses saves these women from the shepherds is the verb used later in Exodus to describe how God will ultimately rescue and save the people of Israel.

Over and over again, the text aligns Moses with God when Moses is paying attention. He notices when something isn't right. He sees the injustices around him, and he can't help but respond—even when it means risking his safety.

The story makes us wonder whether we are paying attention to the suffering around us with the same concern. Are we seeing the injustices in our community and our world? When we do see an injustice, are we tempted to ignore it or respond like Moses? Ultimately, the practice of paying attention cannot leave us where we are. It calls us to action, guided by our confidence in a faithful God who liberates.

> I've never heard tell of a small speck of dust that is able to yell.
> (Dr. Seuss, *Horton Hears a Who!*)

In a timeless classic by Dr. Seuss, *Horton Hears a Who!*, Horton the elephant is going about his daily business, splashing in the pool, when suddenly he hears something out of the ordinary. If he had not been paying attention, he might not have even noticed it. But Horton's curiosity allows him to hear "a very faint yelp as if some tiny person were calling for help." How can that be? he thinks to himself. "I've never heard tell of a small speck of dust that is able to yell." As Horton looks closer, he discovers it is much more than a tiny speck of dust. It is a whole world of tiny little Whos crying out for help.[4] We do not aim to compare any specific community to the fictional Whos down in Who-ville. However, the story does speak to our own inattentional unawareness toward entire communities and systems around us, and it invites us to take the first step toward acting for others by paying attention in ways that we haven't before.

When I (Mary Alice) was living in Waco, Texas, our church would often host the local Homeless Coalition each January as they gathered to do community visits and to collect information for the Point-in-Time Count, which is required to qualify for funding from the US Department of Housing and Urban Development. Every year, a group of social workers, city managers, and nonprofit staff would meet early in the morning at our church and go out in small groups to visit with our houseless neighbors living in different areas of the city. While conducting the survey, the groups would also deliver toiletry items, food, and information about community resources available to people.

One morning, I arrived at church early to help welcome the groups before they left and was invited to join them on their morning route. I expected to visit some tent camps I had seen around town or other areas where I knew people lived downtown and near the interstate. I was shocked when we started driving the same route I drove to work daily. They pointed to wooded areas behind restaurants, alleys behind stores, grassy areas behind warehouses—all areas where they knew people lived or had lived at some point in the past year. I was speechless because I drove past these areas every single day, and I visited many of these businesses regularly, yet I was completely unaware that people were living in houselessness all around me. It made me wonder if I would have noticed this sooner if I had only been paying attention.

The Role of Privilege

We would be remiss to discuss noticing injustice without also acknowledging the role privilege plays in our ability to see clearly. Some are surrounded by such injustice that it is impossible to *not* see it; it affects their everyday life—their every breath. Then there are those who have a choice whether to stop and pay attention to injustice or just to keep walking. That choice is a privilege.

As someone with a physical disability who grew up needing to use a wheelchair and walker to help me (Mary Alice) get around, it was impossible for me to *not* notice when places were inaccessible to me, such as when I could not get to the second floor of my school because there was no elevator. Even today, in my own church, a person in a wheelchair or using a walker cannot sing in the choir loft or speak from the pulpit, because those areas of the sanctuary are inaccessible; it's one of the first things I noticed when I walked into the sanctuary for the first time. These types of inequities are immediately visible to me but often go unnoticed by many nondisabled people because their life situation does not require them to notice. They do not have to pay attention to the availability of ramps and elevators—because their mobility does not require them.

When I was in middle school, I attended an awards ceremony for a statewide speech competition in a school auditorium. One by one, other students walked up the steps onto the stage to receive their awards, and I remember panicking about what I would do if my name were called and how I would get on the stage. Before I could come up with a plan, the emcee of the event announced I had won first place in my age category. My middle-school self was both excited and terrified about what to do next. I rolled in my wheelchair to the front of the auditorium, waving to the person giving out the awards from below the stage, but he kept calling out my name and finally went on to the next part of the program because he thought

I wasn't there. I kept waving my hands in the air and calling to him, "I'm down here!" but he could not see me from where he was standing. No one had considered what to do if a student was unable to climb the steps to receive an award.

A friend of mine who is an activist for disability rights often talks about the challenge of not being able to visit certain restaurants, stores, or businesses with her family because they are not accessible to her and her husband, who are both wheelchair users. As her children grew older, she didn't want them to blame their parents when they couldn't go to a particular place they wanted to visit that wasn't accessible, so she became mindful to help shift the narrative. Instead of saying, "We can't go there because we can't get up the stairs," she was intentional to say, "We can't go there because that place isn't built to include all people."[5]

As the authors of this book, we want to be especially mindful of how our privilege prevents us from noticing injustices that are all around us, too. For instance, as white, cisgender, heterosexual professionals with graduate degrees, the two of us know there are countless things we do not think twice about that our siblings of color and LGBTQ+ siblings think about on a daily basis. If we are not intentional about examining our privilege, we cannot see clearly.

For instance, I (Mary Alice) was refueling my car with gas one day with a Black friend, and he noticed that I did not get a receipt afterward. He said, "Hey, don't you want to go back and get a receipt?" I shrugged and said, "Oh, it's fine; I don't need one." He became quiet and said, "I always get a receipt for gas, and for every big purchase I make." I could not understand why he was being so insistent about a purchase that I made every week until he added, "I always get a receipt because I never want to give anyone another reason to assume that I drove off without paying for it. And if I were ever stopped, they wouldn't take my word for it. They wouldn't believe me like they would you." His words hit me in the gut. That thought would never have crossed my mind. I realized that day that when a situation involving inequity, inequality, or inaccessibility has to be brought to my attention, something which has never crossed my mind before or has gone unnoticed because it has never impacted me personally . . . that is privilege.

Another example: I (Tyler) often find that church people immediately accept my authority as a minister and preacher without comment or question. They are accustomed to a white man in those spaces, so it does not strike them as worthy of comment or special attention. My wife, however, is consistently questioned about her role as an ordained minister. She cannot simply walk into the hospital and assume people will accept her as a clergyperson. She cannot attend a community rally in plain clothes and receive instant acceptance as a faith leader.

Knowing that we carry privilege we might not be aware of, in the process of writing this book we have sought and received feedback from friends and colleagues who would name and call out some of our unconscious biases. One of the biggest examples of this was in one of the first stories of this chapter. The original experiment studying inattentional unawareness involved a person in a gorilla suit walking into the middle of the camera frame, but the participants were so focused on counting the number of times the ball was passed that they completely missed seeing the gorilla. After reading the story, several of our friends of color reminded us of the profoundly hurtful and traumatizing ways that the Black community, and particularly Black women, have been compared to primates and how triggering this example could be, particularly in light of the focus of our book. While it was certainly not at all our intention, neither of us would have even considered how this story might make our Black readers feel, and we changed it immediately.

So as we speak about awakening to unjust situations, we also call ourselves to pay attention in new ways, realizing that it will look different for each of us. We cannot prescribe for you an exact plan for raising awareness; it will depend on your various contexts. Different types of privilege may make it difficult to notice how other people are affected by injustice. We will need to take differing and distinct steps to mitigate the pain we see. We will need to work through the uncomfortable feelings associated with acknowledging privilege. We can only encourage you to begin to look closer and pay deep attention to the life experiences of those who are different from you.

Choosing to pay attention to injustice is a sacred responsibility. It is hard and holy work! When something doesn't seem right, are we noticing, as Moses did? Do we pay attention to the marginalized voices in our community? Do we know their names? Have we listened to their voices and heard their stories?

Seeing What We Can't Not See

Oftentimes, the response of people in places of privilege is that they "didn't know" or "didn't understand" the struggles of those in marginalized communities. All of us are on an unfolding spiritual journey, getting on the train at different points and coming to the station at different times of our lives, yet never fully arriving at the destination. This is especially true of learning about privilege and various types of oppression. We all have weaknesses in our awareness, and none of us can see the world from another's vantage point. However, in the face of pervasive hate, injustice, and evil, and in a world in which we have the capacity to be more connected to one another than ever before, we cannot claim to "not know" about the plights of our neighbors anymore. Not knowing is not an option for people of faith. Of course, we can't know everything about all injustices. That's an unrealistic and unhelpful goal. But if we seek to truly tune in compassionately to the many voices around us, we will inevitably become more and more aware of the ways our neighbors encounter unjust policies and oppressive forces.

The antidote to our ignorance begins with getting to know one another across our differences. According to a 2022 study by the Public Religion Research Institute, across racial groups, core social networks tend to be made up of people of the same race or ethnic background. But there are some distinctions. Among white Americans, 90 percent of their closest friends are also white. However, among Black Americans, 78 percent of their closest friends are Black. And among Hispanic Americans, 63 percent of their most intimate relationships are with people who identify as Hispanic. In other words, white Americans are the most likely group to have racially homogeneous friend groups.[6] An article in the *Washington Post* about a similar study says, "The implication of these findings is that when we talk about race in our personal lives, we are by and large discussing it with people who look like us."[7] How can we begin to know the challenges our diverse neighbors are facing if we're living in such silos?

Womanist theologian the Rev. Dr. Kelly Brown Douglas, in her book *Resurrection Hope: A Future Where Black Lives Matter*, notes that racial proximity is one of the critical steps toward combating our nation's pervasive anti-Black narrative. We need to come close to each other in mutual listening and learning in order to find out about experiences that are different from our own. The Rev. Dr. Douglas, who is dean of the Episcopal Divinity School at Union Theological Seminary in New York City, grounds this admonishment in the ministry of Jesus:

> The proximity to which Jesus calls his followers requires concerted and sustained encounters with the Black experience that do not objectify Black people. Such encounters help foster a re-imagining of the Black body that will lead to eliciting responses of care and kindness as opposed to outrage and fear when encountering Black people in everyday life.[8]

The legacy and current reality of racial segregation make this kind of proximity particularly difficult, but it is not impossible.

The reality is that if we don't know or don't understand, we need to learn. Indeed, we need to do our homework and not expect marginalized people to do it for us. Just as Moses did, we need to leave our familiar surroundings and come close to circumstances and people unfamiliar to us. We need to look one another in the eyes and listen to each other's stories. We need to sit with one another in the pain, discomfort, and weariness. In so doing, we are holding space for God's revolutionary love to seep into our pores and break out of our lives. We are coming to more fully understand and embrace the words of Fannie Lou Hamer: "Your freedom is shackled in chains to mine. And until I am free, you are not free either."[9] As he leaves the comfort of home and learns to pay attention to the experiences of those around him, Moses sees that things aren't right, and he can't return to his comfortable life. We can experience this kind of radical sharing and revolutionary love only if we actually begin to know one another.

"And God Knew"

In a world that does not always understand, continually fails to get it right, and often claims to "not know" the suffering of marginalized peoples, we can trust this: God knows. At the end of Exodus 2, we read:

> After a great many days, the king of Egypt died. And the children of Israel groaned from the slavery and cried for help. Their cry went up to God from the slavery. And God heard their groaning and God remembered the covenant with Abraham, Isaac, and Jacob. And God saw the children of Israel, and God knew. (vv. 23–25)

The new Egyptian ruler, who is introduced without a name in Exodus 1, dies. Yet the Israelites remain enslaved. Their despairing cries reach God, who is listening. God hears their cries and remembers the covenant made with their ancestors. This is the first time God is mentioned in this story; to this point, Moses has been the witness to the injustice of the Hebrews. God did not point out the injustices to him or show up with a big sign to highlight the wrongs. It is Moses' job to see them, and it is our job too.

Lenten Practices

Paying Attention

(Self-Reflection)

Monday

Think of a moment recently when you failed to notice. Maybe it wasn't a person dressed in a chicken suit, but another person, place, or event you didn't observe until someone pointed it out.

Tuesday

Privilege, especially white privilege, can be a difficult topic to explore. Yet people undeniably experience the world in different ways. Think of some examples of privilege in your life. Maybe it is privilege based on your race, gender, socioeconomic status, or physical ability.

Wednesday

Take a moment today to read slowly and intentionally through this week's Exodus passage, 2:11–25. What do you find compelling about this story?

Thursday

Draw an image, write a poem, or do some freewriting concerning Moses and his willingness to pay attention (like God) in this week's Exodus passage.

Friday

Read John 9 and ponder its significance and connection to this week's lesson about seeing in new ways.

Saturday

What prevents you from seeing? Where might you be missing the chicken in the story of your everyday life?

Sharing Together

(Group Discussion Questions)

1. Take time to discuss the challenging subject of privilege with others. Have you benefited in your life from society's acceptance of your race or gender or sexuality or physical ability or class? How do those without those privileges suffer in concrete ways?

2. If your group shares a privileged identity (for example, being male or white or able-bodied or heterosexual) that provides advantages, conduct a "privilege audit." Consider the books you read, the news media you consume, the movies and TV you watch, and the restaurants you support. Think about the leadership of organizations you participate in. How many of these personal and professional contexts are mostly or entirely white or male or nondisabled or heterosexual?

Begin to notice the ways you interact daily with people who are similar to you.

3. Read and discuss the story in Luke 13:10–17 of the healing of the bent-over woman and the example set by Jesus of truly seeing people.

4. Moments of awe and wonder are all around us, if only we pay attention. We are invited to pay attention to beauty in the world but also called to pay attention to pain, difficulty, and injustice. God meets us in those spaces too. Share with the group some of those moments of either awe or pain that you are paying attention to.

Taking Action
(Next Steps)

1. Take time this second week of Lent to learn more about a particular injustice in your community. This action may require you to reach out to people unlike you in some way. One way to focus your attention might be to explore disability justice.

2. Do some research about any local workshops, events, or conferences that focus on justice issues such as racism or LGBTQ+ issues. Make a plan to attend one to learn more. If you can't find one, perhaps your religious community would be open to sponsoring one. If these options do not seem safe or feasible, perhaps you could build relationships across differences in places you already inhabit, such as work or civic groups or volunteer opportunities. Then have one-on-one conversations once trust and an ethics of care have been established.

3. Commit to learning about someone who has experienced marginalization. Read a memoir by a minoritized person or watch a movie or documentary about a marginalized person or community. Check with your library or bookstores, or find resources online. We recommend movies such as *13th* and *Crip Camp* and books such as *Just Mercy* and *Heavy: An American Memoir*.[10]

4. Find some time this week to intentionally pay attention to the present moment. Practice moments of mindfulness—a way of quieting the

mind and tuning in to the present. You can find resources online to guide you. Find a public place to sit and observe your surroundings. What do you hear? What do you see? What do you feel in your body? Try to be with the moment and not the past or future.

5. If you want to learn more about mindfulness, one great introduction to the practice is Bhante Henepola Gunaratana's book *Mindfulness in Plain English*.

Look Again!

Exodus 3 and 4

The Surprise in the Subway

At 7:51 a.m., in the middle of the morning rush hour in Washington, DC, a man got off the Metro, found a clear spot beside a trash can, and prepared to play music for people passing by on their morning commute. He certainly blended in with the crowd around him, wearing blue jeans, a T-shirt, and a Washington Nationals baseball cap. He opened a small case and removed a violin. Then he threw in a couple of bucks and some change, swiveled it around to face the people walking by, and began to play.

For the first several minutes, no one paid him any attention. In fact, sixty-three people walked by without stopping before a man slowed down and paused for a moment to listen to the music. Then he kept walking. After another minute, a woman threw in a dollar bill and continued walking. After about six minutes, someone finally decided to stop and take in the music. However, the man looked at his watch and quickly began to walk away. He was late for work. A three-year-old boy was so mesmerized that he didn't want to move, but his mother tugged him along.

In the forty-five minutes that the musician played, seven people stopped what they were doing to listen to his music, at least for a minute. Twenty-seven gave money, even though they hurried on by, for a total of $32 and some change. Of the 1,070 others who passed by on their morning commute, few even turned to look. And when the man finished playing his music that morning, no one applauded. Most people didn't even notice.

Only one person recognized that this violinist in the subway station was Grammy Award winner Joshua Bell, one of the finest musicians in the world, playing some of the most intricate pieces of music ever written on a violin reportedly worth $3.5 million. Just a few days earlier, Bell had sold out his concert at Boston's Symphony Hall, where average tickets cost $100. Two weeks later, he would play to a standing-room-only audience so in awe of his music that they actually held back their coughs until the applause. However, on that Friday in the subway station, Joshua Bell was just an ordinary street performer.

The scenario was organized by the *Washington Post* as part of a social experiment in 2007. The researchers sought to answer this question: "If a world-famous musician and his $3 million fiddle brought some of history's most beautiful music to a rush-hour crowd, would people stop and listen?"[1] The answer: *Not really*. More than a thousand people passed by without even noticing the blazing bush playing music in the subway station that day.

Of course, we can critique the people in the subway station experiment all we want, but would we have done anything differently? Paying attention requires intentionality, focus, and a deliberate quieting of our minds and souls to be present with what is happening right in front of us. Such hard work is particularly challenging when our minds are pulled in so many different directions toward competing demands.

Throughout this Lenten journey, we are leaning into a different way of going about our day-to-day lives in order to notice God's presence with us and to become aware of the sacred moments that are all around us—including those that are nudging, or even commanding, us to take action. It requires adjusting not only our eyes but also our minds and souls. If we are not paying attention, we could miss what very well may be holy ground.

Holy Ground (Exod. 3:1–5)

> The messenger of the Living God appeared in a fiery flame from the midst of the bramble bush. Moses looked and the bush was burning with fire, but the bush was not consumed. (Exod. 3:2)

Perhaps what Moses discovers in Exodus 3 is the divine possibility of the present moment. In the midst of what would have been an ordinary landscape for him, Moses sees this incredible burning bush. He is not on a spiritual retreat or pilgrimage, hoping to hear a word from God. Moses has not made preparations for such an encounter. He is tending the sheep of his father-in-law, just doing his job, when he encounters the holy. Moses has already learned something on his own about paying attention to what is not right. And now, God comes on the scene.

The story begins in an uneventful way, but the ordinary becomes extraordinary when God's messenger appears in a fiery flame from the midst of the bramble bush in verse 2. The astonished Moses says to himself, "I must turn aside and see what in the world is going on here." The Hebrew word behind the verbal phrase "turn aside" means to change direction or to deviate. Moses sees a strange sight—a bush is on fire, but the fire is not destroying it—and makes the decision not to continue on his way. He cannot go on as if nothing had happened. Moses deviates from his normal routine to see this "great sight" (v. 3).

What would have happened if Moses had not turned aside that day? What if he had been distracted by all of his sheep or so troubled by everything that had happened to him recently that he did not notice the bush burning in the distance? What if he noticed but just kept walking? What if he thought to himself, "I've got way too much going on right now. Pharaoh wants to kill me, I'm a fugitive, and now I've got to take care of all these sheep. There are way more important things going on right now. I don't have time to go on some wild goose chase." Moses has legitimate and numerous reasons to be preoccupied with his responsibilities and obligations.

Moses does not do any of those what-ifs. He stops, turns aside, and takes a closer look. Only after Moses turns aside in Exodus 3:4 does God call out to him. He doesn't hear from God until he makes the choice to stop. He must take time to come into the present moment in order to hear from the holy. In verse 5, God says, "Moses, do not come any closer. Take off your sandals. Because the ground on which you are standing is holy ground." Biblical scholar Terence Fretheim points out,

> Moses' encounter with God takes place far removed from the sights and sounds of the religious community. There is no temple nearby where he might expect a divine appearance, no sign that this is a holy place . . . . Yet it would not be the last time that God appeared to shepherds in the wilderness with an announcement of peace and goodwill. And it would not be the last time that God chose *a nontraditional, nonreligious setting for a hearing for the word.*[2]

Holy ground is sometimes in the least expected places. It certainly is not limited to religious buildings or spiritual spaces. If we are open, holy ground can be found in nontraditional ways and places.

We learned this lesson anew in the midst of the COVID-19 pandemic. Many church buildings were closed for months, and the religious spaces we counted on as sacred were no longer safe or accessible to us. As time passed, we began to discover holy ground all around us. Some people found holy ground on their daily walks through the neighborhood or through spending more time outside at parks. Some baked bread for others as a spiritual discipline, sat down with their immediate families more often for meals, and met some of their neighbors for the first time. We saw the holy ground of our hospitals as health-care and other frontline workers continued to show up and care for our communities in the midst of an anxious time. When the world began to shut down and our daily activities came to a sudden halt, COVID forced some of us to turn aside and be more present to God in the world and the people around us. The question is, will we continue this practice in a post-COVID world?

Wilderness Moments

> And Moses was shepherding the flock of Jethro, his father-in-law, the priest of Midian. And he drove the flock to the wilderness, and he came to the mountain of God called Horeb. (Exod. 3:1)

I (Mary Alice) was leading a small group at my church in Texas in a discussion of this passage in Exodus 3, and I asked the group to tell me about the times they have experienced God in unexpected places. I must admit I was caught completely off guard by their responses. Most of them did not tell me about mountaintop moments in their lives; they told me about their pain. They shared times of disaster, sickness, anxiety, and helplessness. One person said she experienced God's closeness in a hut in South Africa surrounded by AIDS and tuberculosis. Another mentioned an Alcoholics Anonymous meeting in a church basement. One woman said she saw God most clearly in Houston in the aftermath of Hurricane Katrina. Another spoke of the palliative care unit at the hospital as her father was dying.

Carolyn shared stories about her daughter Allie. Allie was in her twenties and living with Vascular Ehlers-Danlos syndrome, an illness that ultimately took her life when she was twenty-three years old. During a challenging time in Allie's illness, she and Carolyn were driving to yet another doctor's appointment. As Allie looked out the car window, she said, "Mom, I see colors differently now. I see the most vivid, beautiful colors that I've never seen before. And I hear music differently, too—I've never heard music this way at any other time in my life. One day, you will see and hear it, too." Carolyn said Allie shared these things with excitement, fully embracing this incredible newness—this ability to see around her what she had never seen before—during what Carolyn knew was the hardest season of her life.

Moses has his divine encounter with God in the middle of the wilderness (3:1), not on fertile ground or in territory he knows well. The name of the place where Moses encounters the burning bush, Mount Horeb, literally means "waste" or "dry"—a place that was dried up and filled with thorns and bushes. It will later become, according to Deuteronomy, the mountain from which God gives legislation to Moses, but for now, it is simply dry and parched land. It is not the location of a sacred site or the hometown of a famous prophet.

The ground that God calls holy is a dry, lifeless wasteland.

There could not be a more accurate name for where Moses finds himself. As a child, he had been taken from his family to be raised in Pharaoh's house. Moses' people are in slavery, so he can't go back "home." Moses had left his comfortable life, awakening to and trying to intervene in the injustices surrounding him. But after killing an Egyptian while trying to save a Hebrew, he became a fugitive hiding from a ruler who wanted him dead. It is no wonder he describes himself in Exodus 2:22 as "a stranger living in a foreign land." Moses has nowhere else to go, and he's not sure what to do next. It is in the middle of the wilderness wasteland of his life that Moses encounters God in a profound way.

What is it about wilderness moments that help us begin to see God in colors, in people, and in ways that we have not seen God before? Maybe it is in the wastelands of our lives, when we are disoriented and things are seemingly in chaos, that other distractions and anxieties begin to fade. In the wilderness, our to-do lists do not seem nearly as important as they do on our regular morning commutes. The everyday stressors of life fall to the wayside, and we are brought to the edge of what matters most and what doesn't matter at all. It is there, on the border between the world we are familiar with and the unknown world we have been thrust into, that we discover face-to-face the sacred presence that has been with us all along.

A dear friend, Brenda, who was like family to me (Mary Alice), was diagnosed with pancreatic cancer in the spring of 2019, just days before Holy Week. She died nine months later. Walking alongside Brenda and her family through that time was one of the most heartbreaking and gut-wrenching tasks I have been entrusted with as a pastor. And yet, those were also some of the most sacred spaces I have encountered. They were hard and they were holy, all at the same time.

Shortly after Brenda's diagnosis, her husband Randall shared the following words with our community in an online journal update:

> There is no doubt that this experience has changed us and is changing us . . . . I'm realizing that our concept of time is now divided into "before the news" and "after the news." Last night, Brenda and I were sitting on the sofa in the hospital room, reflecting on some "before" happenings in our lives. I said, "Don't you just wish that we could go back and resume life where we left it twelve days ago, but live from that moment forward with the awareness of life's value that we have now?" We both shed a few tears before I said, "So what do we do now?" And without even hesitating, Brenda replied, "We live the life we have left with this new reality of the true gift that life really is."[3]

That is exactly what they sought to do every day for the final months of Brenda's life. Hospitality was crucial to Brenda, so her family continued having people over for gatherings and meals in their home as long as they were able. They moved her son's senior voice recital from the Baylor University concert hall to their living room and packed it with his closest friends and family. He sang beautifully—a gift of courage and love for his mom, who sat in the front row and beamed the entire time. They hosted Easter lunch and Thanksgiving dinner that year with close family and friends, and there was not a dry eye in the room as we shared around the table together and savored every bite of Brenda's homemade bread. I remember the night they called me late and said, "We're decorating for Christmas early—come over!" We made homemade hot chocolate and listened to Christmas music, and Brenda told me the stories behind each ornament I pulled out of the box to hang on the tree. It was as if the room just sparkled and glowed that evening—and it had little to do with the lights on the trees. Throughout those nine months with Brenda, our time together became so real. Nothing was left unsaid. It was as if the experience had brought all of us to the edge of life and into a holy space together with no distractions and no pretenses.

At the end of the novel *Gilead* by Marilynne Robinson, Pastor John Ames says,

> It has seemed to me sometimes as though the Lord breathes on this poor gray ember of Creation and it turns to radiance—for

> a moment or a year or the span of a life. And then it sinks back into itself again, and to look at it no one would know it had anything to do with fire, or light." The thing is, he says, "Wherever you turn your eyes the world can shine like transfiguration. You don't have to bring a thing to it except a little willingness to see. Only, who could have the courage to see it?[4]

Perhaps the wilderness moments of life help us muster the courage to see in ways we have never seen before and to hope that God will show up in a bigger way than we could even imagine. Maybe that is where God shows up best.

Holy Spaces Have Holy Consequences

> Now, go, I will send you to Pharaoh to lead out my people, the Israelites, from Egypt. (Exod. 3:10)

A lot of Christians end Moses' story at the burning bush with the encouragement to "turn aside" to see the burning bushes that are all around us. It is certainly an important message: stop and pay attention to God's presence with us in ways we have not before. However, seeing the burning bush is only half the story, the first part of Moses' call to leadership. Moses does not have this incredible experience with God in the wilderness, post a photo of it on his social media with the caption #blessed, and then return to shepherding his sheep! As we've seen, Moses has been paying attention to what's happening around him, how people are suffering, and instinctually acting against injustice. Now, God is showing up in a big way—blazing in the desert—to tell Moses the time has come to make an even more significant commitment.

This story is important because it marks a turning point for Moses—and for the people of God. It is what happens *after* the burning bush that makes this story increasingly significant. His encounter with the burning bush gives Moses the courage to pursue what God is calling him to do next.

In Exodus 3:7–10, God says to Moses, "I have observed the misery of my people." Not just, "Hey, have this moment of awe." The call is to Moses but involves others. Verse 7 notes that God continues speaking; God has more to add to the conversation on holy ground. God has seen the oppression of God's people and desires to deliver them from their bondage. God is sending Moses to lead the process of liberation of God's oppressed children. Seeing the burning bush leads Moses to discover what God is calling him to do next: to go back to Pharaoh to deliver the Hebrews from slavery in the land of Egypt.

What happens in the holy spaces of our lives should also have holy consequences in the world around us. Moses' experience *with* God directly leads to action *for and alongside* God. Spiritual formation and work to bring about social justice cannot happen in vacuums—they naturally flow into and out of one another, fueling the fire and fanning the flame of the Spirit's work and witness in our world. As Richard Rohr points out, Moses' burning-bush moment is "the perfect integration of action and contemplation." His experience with God at the burning bush is immediately followed by a call that has "social, economic, historical, and political implications" in the world around him.[5] Holy spaces demand faithful action.

If we think we can walk away from a burning bush unchanged, we need to look again. This is the challenge issued by the Rev. Ron Bell in the days following the murder of George Floyd in 2020. The Rev. Bell was then the pastor of Camphor Memorial United Methodist Church, which is in an important historically Black neighborhood in St. Paul. After the horrific incident when police officer Derek Chauvin knelt on Floyd's neck for nine minutes and twenty-nine seconds, protests and riots broke out across the St. Paul–Minneapolis area. People across the country watched the news, many of them in shock at the violence, unrest, and chaos destroying the city. The Rev. Bell rightfully called for us to "look again" at what was happening and to look beneath the surface at why it was happening. He writes:

> My city is burning, but not in the way the media is showing. Did you see the fire, not the one burning down the precinct but the one burning in the hearts of the wounded in my community? The grieving mothers and grandmothers recalling the voice of our dear brother George Floyd, as he called for his mother, while taking his last breath. The burning of the hearts of we who

> wept, when our governmental leaders refused to arrest the murderer of this wicked and inhumane deed. Did you see that fire?
>
> Did you see the shattered glass, not those easily replaceable windows scattered in pieces on the ground under our feet? Instead, the shattered glass of expectation for justice, the shattered glass of respect for our humanity that our murderers continue to display, the shattered glass of hope as we watched our brother's body lay, lifeless under the knee of his murderer. Did you see that glass shatter?
>
> You must have witnessed the looting? Not the ones the cameras and social media love to exploit, but instead the looting of our human rights. The looting of our constitutional rights as citizens. The looting of our communities for decades by corporations for greed. Did you see that looting?
>
> I think you were so busy looking for a riot that you missed the gathering of the grieving. I think you were so busy looking for looters that you missed the lament and heartbreak of a community. I think you were so busy looking for trouble that you missed the tragedy of systemic racialized trauma on the bodies of black and brown people. Tonight, tomorrow, and even the next day I beg of you, look again.[6]

In what ways do we need to look again and heed the call for justice from the burning bushes in our world? They are not always hiding off the beaten path. They often are right in front of us—bursting forth and fanning flames in this wilderness wasteland where we find ourselves. Perhaps it is the yard signs and posters crying out that Black Lives Matter or the protester calling out in the streets or the op-ed decrying how Black and brown communities get overlooked in conversations about the need for gun control. These could be the burning bush beckoning us toward justice in our cities and world.

One of our friends and fellow church members, Missy Smith, is a social worker and community activist engaged in the work of antiracism in Louisville. She says that her burning bush is at the exit doors of the Louisville Metro Corrections Office. Each week during the protests after the murder of Breonna Taylor, Missy would sit outside and wait for people who had been arrested while protesting to be released from jail and help them find a safe way home. She shared how each person she encountered on this holy ground helped to fuel her passion for justice in our community.

The Rev. Ron Bell and our friend Missy combine holy attention with holy action in the world. They discern their next steps while standing on holy ground, testifying to the power of burning bushes to call us forward into God's purposes. They suggest to us that these two aspects of spiritual life are woven into each other, almost without distinction.

We need to turn aside. We need to look again. But the work doesn't end there; that is only the beginning. Burning bushes are calling all of us to join with God in the hard and holy work of creating a world where justice and love are abundant.

Elizabeth Barrett Browning wrote,

> Earth's crammed with heaven,
> And every common bush afire with God:
> But only he who sees, takes off his shoes,
> The rest sit round it, and pluck blackberries,
> And daub their natural faces unaware.[7]

We are so accustomed to ignoring what seems common. Are we ready to take off our shoes and get to work? Or are we, too, plucking blackberries, completely unaware of the holy ground beneath us and the holy call before us?

What are the burning bushes around you, and what are they calling you to do next?

Who Am I to Go?

> But Moses responded to God, "Who am I to go to Pharaoh and bring out the children of Israel from Egypt?" (Exod. 3:11)

It is one thing to hear the call from God, but another thing entirely to take the next step forward, particularly when God tells you to start a revolution. When God calls out to Moses from the burning bush in Exodus 3:4, Moses almost immediately responds with the confident words, "Here I am, Lord!" But just moments later, in verse 11, he begins to change his tune from "*Here* am I" to "*Who* am I?" In the verses following this epic, burning-bush moment, Moses comes up with one excuse after another why he doesn't think he's cut out for the job. Even Moses, one of the most heroic figures in the Bible, says things like, "What if the Israelites ask me questions about how exactly all of this is going to go down—what am I supposed to say to them then?" "What if my elders don't believe me or won't listen to me?" "What if I'm not a strong enough speaker to get the words across? I get nervous and my words always get jumbled up. What if I can't say things correctly?" Even as he has become attuned to the injustices against his people, Moses cannot imagine himself going against Pharaoh and taking on a role of this magnitude. Moses may have been experiencing something we now call impostor syndrome.

Psychologist Pauline Clance was the first to recognize and name impostor syndrome in the 1970s. In her work as a therapist, she began to notice a trend among many of the undergraduate students in her practice. Though they had high grades, they often commented that they did not believe they deserved their spots at the university; they just got lucky. Some even thought their acceptance must have been some admissions error. While Clance knew these fears were unfounded, she could remember feeling the same way when she was in college. Clance began to study the impostor syndrome in female college students and faculty. She determined that these women experienced significant feelings of "fraudulence"—as if they couldn't possibly be good enough to be in the positions they were in.

More recent studies show that the syndrome is more common among those who are different from most of their peers, such as women in high-tech careers and first-generation college students. It affects people across the spectrum of gender, race, age, sexuality, and a range of occupations. It is suggested that up to 82 percent of us experience impostor syndrome at some point in our lives.[8]

For example, following the release of *Star Wars: Episode 1*, one of its stars, Natalie Portman, was accepted as a student at Harvard University. But she later said of that experience, "I felt like there had been some mistake, that I wasn't smart enough to be in this company, and that every time I opened my mouth I would have to prove that I wasn't just a dumb actress."[9] Acclaimed novelist John Steinbeck wrote in his journal, "I am not a writer. I've been fooling myself and other people."[10] Sheryl Sandberg, former chief operating officer at Facebook, says of her college experience, "Every time I was called on in class, I was sure that I was about to embarrass myself. Every time I took a test, I was sure that it had gone badly. And every time I didn't embarrass myself—or even excelled—I believed that I had just fooled everyone once again. One day soon, the jig would be up."[11]

Perhaps Moses is experiencing impostor syndrome, too. When people think of the story of Moses, the first thing to come to mind is probably not the moment in Exodus 4 when Moses says, "I don't think I can do this, God. Maybe you should choose somebody else." Nor do we think of a strong woman like Sheryl Sandberg as being insecure or of a great author like John Steinbeck feeling incapable of being a writer. It is a good reminder that we cannot know what feelings of inadequacy people carry beneath the surface. We only see the tip of the iceberg of people's lives and not the underlying struggles, challenges, obstacles, and anxieties hidden beneath the water. Feeling self-doubt when faced with a huge task, like standing up to the powerful on behalf of the oppressed, makes Moses incredibly human.

As many excuses as Moses makes, God responds to every single one. In fact, the majority of Exodus 3 and 4 is a back-and-forth conversation between God and Moses. So often, we would love just one word from God—Moses receives a full conversation in which God offers reassurances and signs of God's presence, helping Moses to work through his trepidations about this divine calling to be God's spokesperson for liberation. God is ever present to the one God calls.

Yet despite the generous way God interacts with Moses over forty verses, Moses comes up with one excuse after another until finally saying, "I don't think I can do this, God. Please just send somebody else" (4:13).

We can critique Moses all we want, but the reality is we probably would have done the same thing. In fact, when I (Mary Alice) look back on some of the times when I have sensed God calling me to take a brave next step in life, my initial response is almost always to list all the reasons why it will not work. There is something within us that so desperately wants to know the big picture for our lives. We want to see where we are headed, and we want to be able to control the narrative along the way. To our frustration, we seldom receive the five- or ten-year plan from God.

But if we are listening, if we are *paying attention,* like Moses, perhaps God will both show us that next step forward and help us gather the courage to take it. When Moses asks God how this plan is supposed to work, God says in Exodus 3:14, "I am who I am." The Hebrew phrase could also mean "I will be who I will be." In other words, God will continue to be present for Moses in this moment and in the future. God reveals God's unique divine name to Moses in the midst of this call as a sign of God's abiding presence and purpose no matter what is to come.

We do not have to have all the answers about where God is leading us next. If we keep waiting for answers, we will never get very far. We can trust God will faithfully be God for us—and God with us—every step of the way. For those of us who struggle with impostor syndrome, we can be reassured as we take those first steps that we are following God's lead. Though Moses asks God to send someone else, we know from the chapters that follow that when Moses walks away from the burning bush that day, he is forever changed. He may not be fully equipped or entirely confident, yet he is courageous, trusting that God will continue to empower him on the journey.

Author Kathy Khang writes, "God knows that Moses has the impostor syndrome—but essentially gives him no room to back out. God enlists the help of Moses' brother Aaron as a wingman, reminds Moses that his shepherd's staff has superpowers, and pushes Moses out of the wilderness."[12] Moses did not know the rest of the story, but he moved anyway. He surely had questions about if and how it would all work out. If he had known there would be rivers of blood, plagues of frogs, long periods of darkness, loss of lives, and years and years of wandering aimlessly in the wilderness . . . would he have gone? In the unknown, God provided all Moses would need to carry out the plan: a companion in his brother Aaron and later Joshua, a power-filled staff, and a pillar of cloud by day and fire by night. With these provisions, Moses kept taking that next brave step forward.

The call to liberation is never pristine. We never feel fully up to the task, aware of all the ways that we are inadequate. God does not promise to fix those inadequacies but does promise God's presence and God's name. God is confident in God's liberating abilities, and Moses is God's human partner—on the ground, getting it done, even with his limitations. And so are we. May we be ready to see this holy ground, recognize the burning bushes blazing bold new trails we have never seen or considered before, and get to work for the God who cries out to us against injustice and says, "Let my people go."

Lenten Practices

Paying Attention

(Self-Reflection)

Monday

How and where have you encountered God in unexpected places? In wilderness moments? In nonreligious settings?

Tuesday

Take a moment today to read slowly and intentionally through Exodus 3:1–15, part of this week's Exodus passage. What do you find compelling about this story?

Wednesday

Where specifically are you finding holy ground this week? What are the barriers or distractions keeping you from noticing the burning bushes around you more often?

Thursday

To what injustices is God calling you to pay more attention? Think about specific areas and incidents in which you notice people are being treated differently in your circles of influence.

Friday

Reflect on an experience where you felt impostor syndrome. What were the circumstances? What was or would have been helpful for you in that situation?

Saturday

One of the greatest gifts of mindfulness training I (Tyler) have found is learning to pay attention, to be aware. One of the definitions of mindfulness by Jon Kabat-Zinn, the creator of the Mindful-Based Stress Reduction program, is "awareness that arises through paying attention, on purpose, in the present moment, non-judgementally."[13] Each of these aspects of the definition is worthy of exploration, but the notion of paying attention is revolutionary. I have found, to my great astonishment, I can walk through much of my day without paying attention, as if I am in a trance. Perhaps even while reading this chapter, you have had to reread a section because your brain naturally started thinking about other matters. I have driven from my office to my home on several occasions without any recollection of the drive. I was not living in the current moment but rehearsing a conversation from earlier in the day, thinking about dinner possibilities or my kids' evening activities. Of course, we need to use our mind sometimes to plan and look to the future. We can't always sit in mindfulness. And we can't pay attention to everything. Yet the practice of mindfulness meditation asks us to step into the present moment, to become aware, to pay attention to this moment—and now, this moment. Explore mindfulness meditation by searching for guided meditations online; Jon Kabat-Zinn, Rhonda V. Magee, Tara Brach, and Devin Berry all provide free meditations.

Sharing Together

(Group Discussion Questions)

1. In Exodus 3:7, God tells Moses that God has observed the suffering of God's people in the land of Egypt. When you observe your community (church, neighborhood, city, etc.), what do you see?

2. Share a time when you experienced impostor syndrome. How did you respond or overcome that way of thinking? How might you engage differently if you took seriously God's presence with you?
3. Continue and expand the conversation from last week about privilege. Enlarge the discussion to think of as many forms of privilege as you can. How have you noticed bias or discrimination against minoritized groups based on these categories?
4. Share stories about times you have noticed the holy breaking into the ordinary. Share ways in which God's transformative power has made itself known in our wildernesses.
5. As a group, read Matthew 4:1–11 and consider Jesus' experience in the wilderness. How does Jesus' experience compare to Moses'? Consider working together to create a communal piece of art concerning the theme of wilderness in one or both of these passages.

Taking Action

(Next Steps)

1. In this chapter, the Rev. Ron Bell calls us to look again at the events around us. Take some time this week to reexamine a news story, particularly one that might be challenging to read because of its disturbing subject matter or jarring point of view. Notice how your body feels.
2. Moses felt insecure and underqualified for the task God had given him, but he was surrounded by significant resources to help him take brave next steps forward. What resources has God entrusted to you or your community to help you to respond to injustice? Make a list.
3. Write down Elizabeth Barrett Browning's verse from this chapter and carry it with you on an adventure of wonder this week. Look around and notice the holy ground all around you, whether in the face of a coworker or the beauty of a tree.
4. Visit a place or space that has been holy ground for you in the past. Pray for the wisdom to connect that holy space to holy action.

Wade in the Water

Exodus 14

Unexpected Roadblocks

A few years ago, Christmas fell on a Sunday, which is always challenging for clergy. I (Mary Alice) finished our Sunday morning service at my former church in Waco, Texas, and drove to the Dallas–Fort Worth airport to fly home to Lexington, Kentucky. I was excited to be home with my family by Christmas night. However, when I got to the airport, two dreaded words flashed across the screen as I was checking in: "Flight canceled."

My heart sank because I knew this was the last flight into Lexington for the day, but I was not giving up. I waited in a long line of disgruntled travelers to see if I could be rebooked to another nearby city. Imagine my joy when they could rebook me on a flight to Louisville leaving in forty-five minutes. I had just enough time to make it through security and get to my gate by boarding time. As I walked down the jet bridge, I quickly called my parents to explain the situation, and my last words to them were, "Don't worry. I'll still be home for Christmas."

The plane took off and, as I am prone to do on airplanes, I quickly fell asleep. I woke about an hour and a half later to a "ding" and a message from the flight attendant saying we would be landing in Louisville in about thirty minutes. My heart began to beat faster because I had almost made it home for Christmas.

A few minutes later, another "ding" and a voice calmly saying, "This is the captain speaking, and unfortunately I have some disappointing news for us this evening." I wondered what she could possibly mean by "disappointing." After all, if the plane were crashing, I don't think the captain would let us know that she had some "disappointing news" for us and to brace for impact. The captain explained that a thick, heavy fog had descended on Louisville, preventing any planes from landing at the airport. The fog was not expected to lift until morning. They had searched all nearby airports, but the fog was widespread. "I am really sorry to tell you this, especially on Christmas," she said, "but we are going to have to turn the plane around and go back to Dallas." What she meant by "disappointing news" hit me in the gut. As the plane began to turn around to make the long trip back to Dallas, I felt a pit in my stomach when I realized I was not going to make it home for Christmas after all—not that night, anyway.

I fully acknowledge that canceled flights are only a minor inconvenience in the larger context of life's challenges. I am grateful for safe travels that night, for a captain who made a difficult decision, and for the flight crew and airport workers who were working hard to take care of us, especially on a holiday. However, I am also not going to wrap up the story with a red bow. I did not magically get home on Christmas night as in a Hallmark Christmas movie. There was no magic sleigh waiting for me when we returned to the airport at midnight. I ate two bags of airplane peanuts for my Christmas dinner and slept in my clothes for about three hours until heading back to the airport for an early flight the next morning.

I imagine all of us have experienced some unexpected hindrance in various seasons of our lives. Sometimes we are forced to stop and go back to square one. In these moments, we are challenged to pay attention to what God is doing and to trust in the Holy One as we take brave next steps.

Keep Still (Exod. 14:1–14)

Last week, we explored Exodus 3–4 and themes of holy ground and holy consequences. At the end of those chapters, we see Moses called and empowered to go to Pharaoh and lead the Israelite people out of

Egypt. Between the event at the burning bush and Exodus 14—our focus in this chapter—God has delivered the Israelites from Pharaoh, a deliverance that comes at the end of a series of plagues (Exod. 7–12) when Pharaoh decides to let God's people go. However, as history has painfully taught us, the end of slavery does not equate to freedom. The Israelites soon find themselves in the wilderness with no idea what to do.

God says to Moses, "Tell the Israelites to turn back and to camp between Migdol and the sea." Turn back? On my plane ride back to Dallas, I could curl up in a ball and go back to sleep, but "turning back" for the Israelites was arduous and confounding. In a seemingly strange turn of events, God decides to "harden Pharaoh's heart" so he will see the Israelites wandering aimlessly through the wilderness and change his mind about their fate. Pharaoh declares he should not have let them go, musters his army with more than six hundred chariots, and pursues the Israelites, intent to corner them in this spot by the sea.

The Israelites see Pharaoh and his army advancing from far away and realize they have nowhere else to go. With the six hundred chariots of Egyptians coming at them from one side and the Red Sea blocking them on the other, they are trapped. Verses 10–12 say that "*in great fear*" they cry out to God, then say to Moses, "Is it because there were no graves in Egypt that you have brought us out here to die in the wilderness instead? What have you done? It would have been better for us to be enslaved in Egypt than to die in this wilderness."

If you study theories on conflict management, you will discover that far too often, when conflict arises, we cannot see beyond what is immediately in front of us. We are quick to pigeonhole ourselves, and others, into either-or scenarios—and in those scenarios, there are winners and there are losers. It is what Franciscan priest and writer Richard Rohr calls "dualistic thinking." He writes, "The old, tired win/lose scenario seems to be in our cultural hard drive, whereas the experience of grace at the core of reality, which is much more imaginative and installs new win/win programs in our psyche, has been neglected and unrecognized by most of Christianity. People who live their entire lives inside of a system of competing, measuring, earning, counting, and performing can't understand how the win/win scenario of the Gospel would even be interesting or attractive."[1] Perhaps this is what the Israelites do when they declare it would be better to be back in slavery than to die in the wilderness, defaulting to a dualistic way of thinking—except in both of those scenarios, they would be losing. Their circumstances are such that they cannot imagine what a win might look like for them; they cannot see anything beyond slavery or death. They cannot imagine what God would do to continue their journey to freedom. Although we know the rest of the story, they had no clue what was about to happen.

The Israelites are often scolded for their "murmuring" in the wilderness—but really, can we blame them? In this moment, however, Moses does not scold them for their anxiety or frustration but turns to the people and says, "Do not be afraid, stand firm, and see the deliverance that God will accomplish for you today. For the Egyptians whom you see today you shall never see again. God will fight for you—and you have only to keep still" (vv. 13–14).

"Do Not Be Afraid, Stand Firm, and See What God Will Do"

In her book *Big Magic: Creative Living beyond Fear,* Elizabeth Gilbert says that whenever fear pops up in her life, she does not try to ignore it or sweep it under the rug. Instead, she makes space for it. "I cordially invite fear to come along with me everywhere I go. I even have a welcoming speech prepared for fear, which I deliver right before embarking upon any new project or big adventure."[2] In her speech to "Dearest Fear," she writes:

> I acknowledge that you believe you have an important job to do in my life, and that you take your job seriously. Apparently your job is to induce complete panic whenever I'm about to do anything interesting—and, may I say, you are *superb* at your job . . . . I recognize and respect that you are part of this family, and so I will never exclude you from our activities, but still—your suggestions will never be followed. You're allowed to have a seat, and you're allowed to have a voice, but you are not allowed to have a vote. You're not allowed to touch the

> road maps; you're not allowed to suggest detours; you're not allowed to fiddle with the temperature. Dude, you're not even allowed to touch the *radio*. But above all else, my dear old familiar friend, you are absolutely forbidden to drive.[3]

"Then," she says, "we head off . . . into the terrifying but marvelous terrain of unknown outcome. It isn't always comfortable or easy . . . but it's always worth it, because if you can't learn to travel comfortably alongside your fear, then you'll never be able to go anywhere interesting."[4] I imagine the Israelites might have found her words helpful, too, in the days following their escape from slavery in the land of Egypt, with no idea of where to go or what to do next in the middle of the wilderness.

God similarly invites God's people forward, in the midst of fear, into a new way of seeing and experiencing. "Do not be afraid" are words often spoken when God reveals God's self in Scripture. For instance, when God calls Abraham and his family to leave their home and follow where God is calling them, God says, "Do not be afraid, . . . I am your shield" (Gen. 15:1). When Hagar runs away from Sarah into the wilderness, the angel of the Lord says, "What troubles you, Hagar? Do not be afraid" (Gen. 21:17). When the shepherds are in the field, keeping watch over their flocks by night, the angel tells them, "Do not be afraid, . . . I am bringing you good news of great joy" (Luke 2:10).

In all of these instances, "do not be afraid" includes a message that God is about to do something completely, unexpectedly good—something we might miss out on if fear and anxiety is at the forefront of our minds. Fear can come along for the ride, but fear must stay in the backseat, and it is absolutely forbidden to drive.

This is not to say that fear is bad or wrong. For most of us, when a threat comes onto the scene around us, our automatic fear response kicks into gear. Both humans and animals have a part of the brain called the amygdala, a cluster of cells about the size of a grape, which is constantly scanning the environment for potentially dangerous situations, always ready to sound the alarm in times of need. The amygdala is an incredibly important part of our bodies, as it keeps us safe and helps protect us from harm when there is not time to think. It is what activates the fight-or-flight response, a discharge of the sympathetic nervous system giving us the energy needed to either fight the threat or flee the scene. The squirrel dashing across the sidewalk and the deer sprinting through the woods have an amygdala that is no different from our own. Without it, animals have been known to play with venomous snakes as a child might play with a toy. They bat at the snakes' hissing tongues without considering the threat.

The amygdala is needed for rare and specific circumstances in which we are truly in danger. Yet sometimes, when we are perpetually anxious or fearful, our amygdala goes into overdrive. Reporting on the comments of Bruce McEwen, a neuroendocrinologist, Peter Steinke writes that when fear overwhelms us, "stress limits our repertoire of responses. Fixated on what is endangering us, we forfeit our imaginative capacities. We act with a small and sometimes unproductive repertoire of behaviors. With fewer alternatives, we act foolishly. When the amygdala is in control, our perception warps measurably. Our mind is set in imaginative gridlock, we obsess about the threat, and our chances of changing our thinking are almost nonexistent. Reactive forces rule."[5]

In the midst of their traumatic situation, the Israelites have every reason for fear and anxiety. The fight-or-flight response has been their only method of survival under Pharaoh's rule, but God instructs the Israelites not to give in to reaction. Rather, they are to "stand firm," so they might see what God will do. After all, if they run or if they fight, they may completely miss out, or they may even get in the way. Instead, they are to stay grounded, trusting in God's presence with them, and to watch expectantly for what's about to happen next.

Did you notice how many times the verb "to see" is in this text? Three times. "See the deliverance that God will accomplish for you today. For the Egyptians whom you see today you shall never see again" (Exod. 14:13). What God is about to do will force the Israelites *to see* things differently than ever before. They are challenged to see beyond what is directly in front of them in order to envision what God will do next. We find here another invitation to pay attention, to slow down and see. It is this quality of sight that helps us see the big picture and act for a bigger purpose and not from a sense of fear.

A few years ago, I (Mary Alice) heard author Anne Lamott speak, and I will never forget the illustration she used about the ways we aimlessly and anxiously wander through this world. She said, "My pastor said you can trap bees on the bottom of mason jars without lids because they don't look up, so they walk around bitterly bumping into the glass walls."[6] I wonder if that was what the Israelites were doing here. They had hit a wall and could not see any alternative to going back to where they came from. When we hit a wall, or a hindrance, Lamott reminds us to slow down and stop the train that keeps us running and frenzied. "Look up. Secret of life," she says. Or in Moses' words, "Do not be afraid, stand firm, and see what God will do."

We are not saying that if we do this, we will find hindrances are simply "blessings in disguise." They are hard, frustrating, and sometimes gravely disappointing. In justice work, we encounter these roadblocks frequently. The road toward justice far too often feels like a dance of one step forward, two steps back, tempting us to throw our hands in the air in defeat. Furthermore, the road to justice can also be dangerous, containing the real threat of violence, especially for people in marginalized communities. However, encountering roadblocks forces us to reimagine what God can do in a situation—to look beyond what is right in front of us to see how God might work in ways that are more expansive than we would ever consider. As Martin Luther King Jr. reminds us, "We shall overcome because the arc of the moral universe is long, but it bends toward justice."[7]

The Lenten season provides an invitation to tune into this reality that King is talking about. During this season, we awaken to God's work in the world; we look for the signs of justice springing up wherever we go.

Crossing the Red Sea Is a Joint Effort (Exod. 14:15–31)

What happens next in the story is quite surprising. God turns to Moses and says, "Why are you crying out to me?" While it may seem like a minor detail, why would God rebuke Moses for crying out to God?

Perhaps it's because God has already told Moses and the Israelites what to do—to trust the God who delivered them from Pharaoh in the night, the God who has already shown them, time and time again, that God can do impossible things, and to be willing to follow this God by day and by night. God is saying to Moses and to the people, I am already doing my part, but there are parts that only you can do here. "Why do you cry out to me?" God says. "Tell the Israelites to go forward."

Notice that the instruction to go forward comes before any mention of Moses using his staff to part the waters of the sea, before any indication of what is going to happen next. This story has been told so often that we are prone to miss an important element: God asks the people to make the first move! We tell this story from Exodus as a miraculous moment of God's divine intervention, but the text reminds us that it is just as much a story of a people who are willing to say *yes* to God—a people who are brave enough to take the next step in following God even when they can't see what's next. Old Testament scholar Terence Fretheim says, "As has been the case throughout the exodus narrative, God does not work alone; God works through the instrumentality of both human and nonhuman powers to accomplish the divine purpose."[8] The hope of the exodus is a joint effort. It is a people co-laboring with God—stepping out in faith together and trusting God to lead the way forward.

The ancient rabbinic tradition emphasizes the initiative of God's people by telling a midrash—a form of ancient Jewish commentary—about an Israelite called Nachshon. According to tradition, the people were a little hesitant to jump into the water. Who would go first? But Nachshon was ready. Even though he could not swim, he waded first into the sea. He trusted God by jumping into the water even before it started to dry up. In fact, according to the midrash, he went farther and farther into the water until it almost completely covered him! In response to his trust, God then parted the waters for the Israelites. This extrabiblical story highlights the people's initial response to God. It is not about Moses' uplifted staff; it is about the people's actions. Author Brian McLaren writes:

> We hear the call to go forward not after the sea has opened, but before. The call to get moving comes not after the way is clear, but while it still seems impassable. The call to join in a

> great migration . . . comes not when we have everything figured and settled and made certain, and not when all obstacles have been removed, but before, when chaos, uncertainty, and turmoil prevail, and when the tumultuous sea shows no sign of parting. Only in that impossible, uncertain, disruptive place . . . does a new depth of naked, essential faith in God mysteriously become possible.[9]

We are invited to see beyond what is directly in front of us and to remember God's presence among us. We then can take action based on this alternative quality of sight.

The Moses of Her People

It was this kind of active faith in liberation that Harriet Tubman lived by—which led to her being called the Moses of Her People. Artist Carl Dixon created a powerful representation of Harriet Tubman and Moses side by side in the carved wood painting he called *Exodus: Journeys of Liberation.*[10] On the left side of the carved painting, Moses with his staff in hand leads the people of Israel through the Red Sea, which has been divided to allow them to walk across it. In the corresponding image on the right side, Harriet Tubman watches as people seeking freedom on the Underground Railroad approach the banks of the Ohio River. The Red Sea and the Ohio River.

Tubman's propensity to step out in faith began at a young age. When she was only five years old, she was rented out as a nursemaid and was whipped every time the baby in the family cried. At the age of twelve, she saw one of her masters prepare to throw a heavy weight at an enslaved man who had tried to escape. Tubman bravely stepped in front of the man, and the weight struck her head instead, leaving her to deal with severe headaches and narcolepsy over the course of her life.

When two of Tubman's brothers, Ben and Henry, discovered they were going to be sold, Tubman began formulating a plan for the three of them to escape. Several of their sisters had already been sold farther south, and she was not going to lose her brothers, too. However, halfway through their escape, Ben and Henry became scared of what might lie ahead. The risk, they said, was just too great, and they decided to go back. Tubman remarkably made the rest of the journey on her own.

She finally crossed into Pennsylvania and found work in Philadelphia, but she did not stay there long. She was not satisfied living free while so many of her friends and family were still in slavery. She put her life on the line, time and time again, to return to the South to help more people escape. Her success became so well-known that owners of the enslaved soon posted a $40,000 reward for her capture or death, but even that didn't stop her.

In 1850 the Fugitive Slave Act allowed fugitive and free enslaved people in the North to be captured and enslaved again. This made Harriet's work that much harder and forced her to lead people even farther north, to Canada. Nevertheless, she persisted. She went on to participate in the Civil War—not only as a nurse, but also as a secret agent and military leader of a Union battalion in a raid against a plantation in South Carolina that freed approximately seven hundred enslaved people.

"She was an illiterate woman of colour" who was "not only physically challenged but disabled by her race and gender," says Catherine Clinton, author of a biography of Tubman. [11] And yet, during a ten-year span, she made more than a dozen trips back into the South, and it is believed she personally helped at least seventy enslaved people escape to freedom, including her elderly parents.[12]

We have few quotes from Tubman, because not much was written about the life of a Black woman at the time, but the following words attributed to her powerfully capture her mission as well as this story of courageous action from Exodus. She said, "I always told [the Lord], 'I trust you. I don't know where to go or what to do, but I always expect you to lead me,' and He always did."[13]

Even before the waters had begun to part, Tubman trusted God to show her the way. Oral tradition tells how she used the song "Wade in the Water" to guide freedom seekers on the Underground Railroad: its coded language warned them to jump in the river, to "wade in the water," whenever people were hunting them so that dogs couldn't trace their scent. And day after day, year after year,

Tubman led people to wade through the water and the wilderness, calling them to take that next brave step forward toward freedom.

The Seas That Have Not Opened before Us

Of course, as Harriet Tubman experienced, when we take the first step toward justice, it often does not feel anything like dry ground beneath our feet. The ground may be covered by water when we step into it. As it did for Nachshon the Israelite, the water may even feel deeper and deeper. There are real risks to jumping into the water before the seas have opened! And those of us who are on the margins often experience these risks to an even greater extent. Those of us in places of privilege would do well to continually remind ourselves of this, and to put ourselves in places of greater risk for and with our marginalized siblings, knowing that some of us have more lifesavers or rafts accessible to us than others do. Some of us can afford to wade into the waters until we are up to our shoulders, while others may not be able to risk wading in above their ankles. Steps toward justice look different for different people.

The words of John Lewis, the late Civil Rights activist and congressman, give us encouragement in these moments: "Do not get lost in a sea of despair. Be hopeful, be optimistic. Our struggle is not the struggle of a day, a week, a month, or a year, it is the struggle of a lifetime. Never, ever be afraid to make some noise and get in good trouble, necessary trouble."[14] With a sixty-year history of Civil Rights activism, Lewis was well acquainted with the risks and results of "good trouble." He was repeatedly arrested and beaten for participating in sit-ins at lunch counters and Freedom Rides across the South. He would go on to help lead one of the most significant marches of the American Civil Rights Movement, from Selma to Montgomery in Alabama, which was temporarily halted on what became known as "Bloody Sunday" as police officers on horseback released tear gas on the protesters and brutally attacked them with clubs and whips. Even with a fractured skull, Lewis spoke to reporters and called upon President Lyndon B. Johnson to take action. Good trouble may sound enticing, but it doesn't come without significant consequences. John Lewis felt that the risks were necessary in order to create change. Each of us will need to discern our steps as we risk wading into the waters.

During Lent, we cultivate qualities of sight, like Moses, Harriet Tubman, and John Lewis, to help us perceive beyond and endure the obstacles and real risks that come with good trouble. This awareness aids us to keep taking these steps as we wade deeper into these troubled waters with God. How might God be challenging you to jump in the deep end, or to make some waves in the shallow end, and to get into some "good trouble"? We are reminded by an old song to wade into the waters. Why? Because "God's gonna trouble the water"! May we find our own ways toward troubled waters too.

Lenten Practices

Paying Attention
(Self-Reflection)

Monday

How would you depict artistically the crossing of the sea as a joint effort between God and God's people? Perhaps sketch or draw some ideas.

Tuesday

Reflect on areas in your life where the seas have not opened yet for you or your community. We can become weary and overwhelmed. We can be anxious and afraid. We cannot see an end in sight and are desperately searching for a way forward. How do you respond in these situations?

Wednesday

Slowly and intentionally read this week's focal passage, Exodus 14. What do you find compelling about this story? What verses draw your attention or make you feel something?

Thursday

Reflect on this prayer, written by Rabbi Stephanie Kolin and shared in the book *The Great Spiritual Migration* by Brian McLaren.[15] Reflect on this idea that "if it can happen once, it can happen over and over and over."

> God Who Creates, God Who Redeems,
> God of shalom—of peace, God of *sh'leimut*—of wholeness,
> We remember standing at the shore of the sea, afraid,
> Our enslavers in hot pursuit, ready to take us back to captivity.
> We remember the tumultuous sea before us that showed no signs of parting.
> And we remember you told us: *v'yisa'u*—go forward.
> We stepped forth. The waters parted.
> We moved our bodies from slavery to freedom.
> You moved our souls from oppression to redemption.
> God who Creates, God who Redeems,
> If it can happen once, it can happen over and over and over.
> *V'yisa'u.*
> Let us cross the sea with all who are enslaved, with captors on their heels.
> And together, let us make those waters part!

Friday

Read Isaiah 43:1–2 and explore its connection to the exodus story. When have you been in deep waters and felt God's presence with you?

Saturday

How is God specifically inviting you to get into some "good trouble"? What would that look like for you today? What local organizations are doing work in this area, and how might you participate?

Sharing Together

(Group Discussion Questions)

1. As a group, look at artist Carl Dixon's carved wood painting *Exodus: Journeys of Liberation*. What do you see in the painting? What draws your attention, and why?
2. Research different versions of Sojourner Truth's speech "Ain't I a Woman?" Where do you see fight or flight in the speech? Why do you

think the speech was reported so differently by different people? How was Truth trying to lead people into "good trouble"?

3. Discuss the idea of "good trouble" and how people with less privilege have to think more deeply about the potential consequences of getting into "good trouble."

Taking Action

(Next Steps)

1. What action might you take during this fourth week of Lent to bring you closer to the lived experience of marginalized communities? Find organizations and people in your community that already engage in this work. How might you counter the segregation our society currently upholds in which many of us operate in homogeneous networks? Begin a process of expanding your social network.
2. It can be tempting to engage marginalized communities on one occasion for a specific purpose. It is much more difficult to create an intentional relationship. How might you commit to an intentional, long-term, and ethical connection to marginalized communities instead of a one-time, surface-level relationship?
3. Learn more about LGBTQ+ religious resources. We recommend the organization Believe Out Loud. See their website: https://www.believeoutloud.com/resources/.
4. Find inspiration for getting into "good trouble" by reading John Lewis's 1998 autobiography, *Walking with the Wind: A Memoir of the Movement*.

Finding God on Day 2

Exodus 16:2–30

The Messy Work of Day 2

We do not often remember the middle of a story. For instance, a movie can begin with an incredible opening scene we will never forget, or the first lines of a book can captivate us and immediately draw us in. Likewise, the ending can tie things together in a way that leaves us feeling satisfied, or it can be so shocking that we cannot click "next episode" fast enough on our Netflix queue. But I cannot think of a single book, movie, or story about which I would say, "Wow, wasn't the middle of the story just incredible."

The middle is often where things begin to fall apart. The way forward is no longer clear. Trust is broken and relationships become complicated. In other words, the middle is where things get messy. We long for a world of adventurous beginnings and fairy tale endings, but we would rather not go through what happens in the middle in order to get us from point A to point B.

We cannot avoid or escape the middle parts of our stories, as painful or difficult as they may be. Brené Brown, a professor and researcher of shame, vulnerability, and empathy, says, "The middle is messy, but it's also where the magic happens."[1] She was in the midst of leading a three-day training through her organization when she realized that no matter where she was or with whom she was working, the middle day of the training, day 2, would always get messy and was by far the most challenging day for everyone involved. Finally, some of the facilitators started asking her if they could rewrite the curriculum, because they really wanted to skip the material for day 2. That was when it dawned upon her: day 2 represents this messy middle kind of work we often want to avoid. It's a self-revealing moment of honesty.

Day 2, she says, is "when you're 'in the dark'—the door has closed behind you. You're too far in to turn around, and not close enough to the end to see the light." In her work with veterans and members of the military, she says, "they know it as 'the point of no return'—an aviation term coined by pilots for the point in a flight when they have too little fuel left to return to their originating airfield."[2]

To put it in simpler terms, it is like what happens when we are going on a bear hunt, as the old children's rhyme goes. No matter what we come up against, we can't go over it. We can't go under it. We can't go around it. We've got to go through it. As much as we want to escape it, the middle is nonnegotiable.

We can't skip day 2 of our stories.

In many ways, we are on day 2 of the work for justice within our world. In the midst of a long-overdue racial reckoning in our country, the fight for women to have a seat at the table, the work to protect the rights of the LGBTQ+ community, the striving to create a world accessible and equitable for people of all abilities, we cry out, "How long, O Lord?" It is the messy middle. Many have made the commitment and begun the work, but now what? In fact, for some who have been fighting for justice for a long time, it may feel like a perpetual day 2. It may be difficult, but let us acknowledge where we are, name the chaos of the middle, and remember that while we cannot skip over it, day 2 is never the end of God's story.

Complaining in the Wilderness

Exodus 16 is metaphorically day 2, where we find the Israelites in the wilderness. It has been almost two months since God delivered the people of Israel from slavery under the rule of Pharaoh and parted the waters of the sea so the Israelites could march through on dry ground to the other side. These events were wonderful and miraculous, but in Exodus 16, the Israelites find themselves in the middle of the wilderness, without food or water, unsure of what is next, and worried about how they are going to survive. Their situation on day 2 is dire, and there is no day 3 in sight.

And so they begin to complain. People often poke fun at the complaints of the Israelites, accusing them of being whiny. From the outside looking in, we could say, "Come on! Have these people lost all faith? Look at all the incredible ways God has provided for them just verses before. Do they not trust God to take care of them anymore?"

It is easy to criticize while not in the wilderness with them—on foot—with no food and no place to call home. Perhaps the Israelites are less pathetically whiny and more realistically human. The Urban Dictionary, an online dictionary of slang, would describe them as "hangry"—the feeling of being so hungry that we become irritable and angry. The Israelites are hangry and scared.

To judge the Israelites for their bad attitudes would suggest that complaining has no place in our life with God, which is not true. The book of Psalms gives voice to many complaints about experiences of abandonment, suffering, grief, and fear. Job freely expresses his complaints against God. And from the cross, Jesus cries out in a voice of complaint: "My God, my God, why have you forsaken me?" When we judge the Israelites, we tend to distance them and their experiences from our own. But we too have the ability to act in this same manner.

Dr. Elna Solvang, professor of religion at Concordia College, says, "At its core, complaint is a turning *to* God—not away."[3] Offering a complaint shows a willingness to be completely open and utterly vulnerable with God about our deepest needs. It also demonstrates courage to name in lament a situation as not fully just. We recognize in the complaint that the world is not how it should be. Complaint then becomes a form of paying attention and being willing to see what is true and not ignore it. If you find yourself needing to offer a word of complaint to God, know there is space for that. There is space for complaint in Scripture and in the history of the people of God.

Every year during the season of Advent, our congregation at Highland Baptist Church in Louisville creates a memorial on our front lawn filled with white crosses in memory of everyone killed by acts of violence within our city that year. It is a demonstration of public lament for and with our city as each year we continue to experience record-breaking numbers of homicides. It was especially harrowing in 2020 when we created more than 140 crosses, including the names of Breonna Taylor and several others who were engaged in various ways in the local protests: David McAtee, a Black restaurant owner who was shot by the National Guard; Tyler Gerth, a local photographer shot at Injustice Square; and Travis Nagdy, one of the most vibrant and energetic local leaders of the movement. More than 71 percent of the homicide victims in 2020 were Black, and 75 percent were under the age of thirty-four.

We hope the crosses on the lawn offer a sacred space in our city during what is supposed to be "the most wonderful time of year" for people also to turn aside, to see and remember the pain, heartbreak, and loss so many in our community are experiencing. However, this practice of paying attention and offering prayers of complaint at our street corner must extend to action far beyond the Highlands neighborhood. Otherwise, our prayers are merely platitudes. We cannot participate in this public act of lament without it moving us to do prophetic work for justice. Lauren Jones Mayfield, associate pastor at Highland Baptist Church, and I (Mary Alice) cowrote in the *Louisville Courier-Journal* in 2020,

> For Christians, this holiday season includes waiting on the birth of Jesus, a holy child who comes to teach us the way of peace through justice and love. Born into political upheaval in the first century, Jesus knows about bearing light among corrupt systems of darkness. He comes to us now in 2020, once again bearing light amidst the darkness of gun violence, systemic racism, generational poverty, and unjust laws. And we need that light more than ever before this year. On our front lawn are over 140 reasons why.[4]

God Provides Manna

The beautiful thing is that God hears the Israelites' complaints in the wilderness—the text reminds us of this four times. God not only hears, but God also provides what the Israelites need, right in the middle of their day 2. There is enough for all of them to eat and be full, every morning and every night. God sends quail to eat in the evening, and in the morning, a thin, flaky substance called manna that looks like frost covering the ground.

If you have wondered what manna actually is, you are in good company. The Israelites must have asked themselves the same thing, because the Hebrew word, *man-hu,* literally means "What is it?"

Reporting on a discovery almost one hundred years ago, a 1927 article in *Time* magazine identified the thin, flaky substance that appeared each morning as the secretion of plant lice that feed on certain shrubs in the Sinai desert. These bugs excrete juice that dries and becomes a flaky coating rich in sugars and carbohydrates. It decays quickly and tends to attract other types of bugs, so you would not want to gather more than a day's worth.[5]

Some might hear this description and ask if it takes away from the miraculous nature of manna in the exodus story. Barbara Brown Taylor asks in return:

> Does manna have to come out of nowhere in order to qualify as a miracle? Or is the miracle that God heard the complaining of hungry people and fed them with bug juice—with food it would never have occurred to them to eat? . . .
>
> How you answer those questions has a lot to do with how you sense God's presence in your life. If your manna has to drop straight out of heaven looking like a perfect loaf of butter-crust bread, then chances are you are going to go hungry a lot . . . .
>
> If, on the other hand, you are willing to look at everything that comes to you as coming from God, then there will be no end to the manna in your life . . . . Nothing will be too ordinary or too transitory to remind you of God . . . .
>
> Because . . . the miracle is that God is always sending us something to eat. Day by day, God is made known to us in the simple things that sustain our lives.[6]

What is God sending you to eat today? What is sustaining you on day 2 of your journey? Do we notice the daily bread right in front of us—whatever it may be? In the moment we often cannot see how

God is taking care of us. We are too close to it. More often than not, it is only when we look back that we see how God's faithfulness has been with us all along.

Rest Is Resistance

Something surprising happens when the people of God go outside to gather manna on the seventh day, the Sabbath day; there is no more food. They assumed the manna would appear daily, and even though they gathered twice the normal amount the day before, they are still surprised to not find any that morning. God has to remind the people of the principle of Sabbath. They do not need to gather on this day; the day is set aside for rest. God has given the people this day of rest.

It is especially jarring for us to see this invitation for the Israelites to rest in the middle of the wilderness. They are in crisis! Likewise, when we constantly feel the weight of the injustices and crises in our world today, the invitation to Sabbath feels completely oppositional to our work. It is tempting to think of Sabbath as a luxury, that is, something we do when we have extra time to spare. We feel guilty for pausing to rest when so much in our world needs to be done. How can we rest in light of the injustices and inequities in our world? How can we truly rest when the forces at work against us seem so relentless?

Recently, I (Mary Alice) was intrigued to see an encouragement to rest where it felt completely out of place—at the Breonna Taylor exhibit at the Speed Art Museum in Louisville. I went to the exhibit, titled "Promise, Witness, Remembrance," and reflected on Breonna Taylor's life, her death in 2020, and the protests that followed, both in Louisville and around the world.[7] There were incredible displays, stunning photographs, and moving works of art throughout the exhibit, including a beautiful portrait of Breonna by Amy Sherald, the artist who painted the official portrait of former first lady Michelle Obama that was unveiled in 2018. But one thing that particularly caught my eye in the exhibit was a small sign in the corner of the room. It said, "As you move through the Promise, Witness, Remembrance exhibit, you might feel the need for a moment of care or a moment of rest." And, if that were the case, you could text the word REST to the number provided to receive a guided meditation from the Nap Ministry.

I had never heard of a "nap ministry," and for a moment I wondered if I had chosen the wrong profession! But I also wondered—especially given the focus of the exhibit—why there would be an invitation to rest? Why not the challenge to get to work? I thought, shouldn't there be names of local justice groups with whom to partner and work in our community? Places to donate money? Ways to join the resistance? I felt a strong dissonance between the invitation before me and the rest of the exhibit around me. It was not until I went home and researched more that I stopped and realized the irony of it all; to rest in the face of injustice *is*, indeed, an act of resistance.

The Nap Ministry was begun in Atlanta by a young Black woman, Tricia Hersey, as a prophetic act of resistance against despair.8 In 2013, she had just enrolled as a seminary student at Emory University, and her schedule was intense. She woke up at 3 a.m. to study, left her apartment by 6 for her 8 a.m. classes, and sometimes would not get home until after midnight. Hersey was also a single mom to her six-year-old son. Making it all the more challenging, she felt overlooked by her seminary colleagues and was deeply affected by the constant news of police brutality against Black communities. She became active in the Black Lives Matter movement and a key leader on the front lines in Atlanta protesting for justice. Then she was robbed one day while walking home with her son, losing all of her classwork, including a sermon—her first—that she was due to preach that week.

At that point, Hersey was ready to quit school and give up. But something else happened instead. She began napping—throughout the day, all around campus, wherever she could find a relatively peaceful space, be it the library or a chapel pew. "I was healing," she said. "Naps really saved my life in that way."[9] For her, naps are more than physical rest. "Sleep is such a vulnerable place," she says. "You have space to talk and vent, to hope, to dream. You can work things out you can't work out when you're awake."[10] She began to research and draw connections between the deep, spiritual healing of rest and resistance to the forces of oppression. She notes that "these toxic systems" disconnect us from each other and tell people that their value can only be found in overworking and constant productivity; how can people resist if they are exhausted?[11] She began to guide local justice groups through meditations and nap talks, such as the one she provided for the Speed Museum.

Jesus also knew about the power of rest and renewal. Jesus knew the powers and principalities he was up against. He knew the constant needs of the world around him. And yet, perhaps as an act of resistance seemingly foolish to everyone else, even Jesus stopped to rest. Jesus went off to be by himself to pray, even when people still needed his help and came looking for him (Mark 1:35). Jesus slept in the bottom of the boat, even when a storm was raging and the disciples thought they were going to drown (Matt. 8:23–27; Mark 4:35–41; Luke 8:22–25). Jesus took time to rest in ways that were shocking and at times infuriating to those who were following him. And he offers us this same invitation: "Come to me, all you who are weary and are carrying heavy burdens, and I will give you rest" (Matt. 11:28). During this Lenten season, how might we see sleep and rest as a contemplative practice for the nurturing of our spiritual life?

Sabbath

The invitation for the Israelites to rest in the wilderness was a new concept after their former life in slavery, working themselves to death in the land of Egypt. Walter Brueggemann notes that we have no evidence Pharaoh took a day for rest or allowed his workers to do the same.[12] Pharaoh forced a relentless lifestyle on the Israelites, and the wilderness offers its own set of relentless challenges. Suddenly, the Israelites are faced with the question, Are we going to trust in the skills and strength we developed for ceaseless work and striving throughout slavery? Or, when everything else has been stripped away from us, are we going to stop and rest, and trust in God to provide?

Perhaps we are faced with a similar question in our modern-day wildernesses, and more often than not, we choose working and striving over resting. In his book *Sabbath: Finding Rest, Renewal, and Delight in Our Busy Lives,* Wayne Muller says,

> Our culture invariably supposes that action and accomplishment are better than rest, that doing something—anything—is

> better than doing nothing. Because of our desire to succeed, to meet these ever-growing expectations, we do not rest. Because we do not rest, we lose our way. We miss the compass points that would show us where to go, we bypass the nourishment that would give us succor. We miss the quiet that would give us wisdom. We miss the joy and love born of effortless delight. Poisoned by this hypnotic belief that good things come only through unceasing determination and tireless effort, we can never truly rest. And for want of rest, our lives are in danger.[13]

Muller points out that this sense of constant striving and never-ending work isn't just a personal problem. It affects our communal work for justice as well: "It colors the way we build and sustain community, it dictates the way we respond to suffering, and it shapes the ways in which we seek peace and healing in the world."[14] He notes that in a career in community development, health, and criminal justice, he has seen, time and time again, that "the way problems are solved is frantically, desperately, reactively, and badly. Despite their well-meaning and generous souls, community and corporate leaders are infected with a fearful desperation that is corrosive to genuine helpfulness, justice, or healing."[15] This description does not sound restful or sustainable!

Throughout this Lenten study, we have talked about how the work toward justice is hard and lifelong. People in places of privilege are eager for a quick fix or an easy solution, wanting to check "ending systemic racism" off the to-do list and move on to other items on the agenda. However, the injustices named throughout this book are complex, intersectional, entrenched, and multilayered. They are the result of generations of faulty systems at work. None of them is going to be fully resolved within our lifetimes. The challenge and invitation is to allow ourselves to become uncomfortable enough to take brave steps forward, and to be willing to get into good trouble, while remembering to rest and take care of ourselves along the way. We need to remember Cole Arthur Riley's words: "Rest is not the reward of our liberation, nor something we lay hold of once we are free. It is the path that delivers us there."[16] The work of justice is far too important for us to lose steam and burn out along the way. Sabbath, then, becomes an intentional faith practice to curb our desire for an easy solution and allows us to maintain our presence and participation in the work of justice as we seek long-term answers.

Not Going Back to Normal

As we began writing this book during the height of the COVID-19 pandemic, so many of us experienced a deep longing to "go back to normal." However, just as Moses warned the Israelites who begged to go back to the only "normal" life they had ever known, slavery in Egypt, a modern-day prophet rose up among us and said the words many of us didn't want but also needed to hear: we would never go back to "normal" again. In the midst of what felt like a very long day 2 of the pandemic, activist and author Sonya Renee Taylor shared on social media, "We will not go back to normal, because normal never was. Our pre-corona existence was not normal other than we normalized greed, inequity, exhaustion, depletion, disconnection, rage, hoarding, hate and lack. We should not long to return my friends. We are being given the opportunity to stitch a new garment. One that fits all of humanity and nature."[17]

The pandemic changed the world, and we cannot go backward. It is the lesson and message of day 2 that when we are too far in and we cannot go back, the only option is to go forward. The question is, how will we go forward in a way that doesn't repeat history but that stitches a new garment for all of humanity? And what stitching skills are we developing in the wilderness that can help usher us into the promised land?

Those of us who have experienced the comforts of privilege can feel the urge to withdraw from the discomfort and messiness of day 2 when it becomes obvious that injustices won't resolve quickly. But the pain and discomfort doesn't mean we are going the wrong direction; it means we are helping to create something new that fits all people, and the old, broken system is not enough. Day 2 during this Lenten season becomes the time to continue to hone our spiritual practices—to balance action with practices of rest and reliance on God's provision, knowing that we are limited, cannot do it all, and need to sustain ourselves spiritually, emotionally, and physically through the journey.

Lenten Practices

Paying Attention
(Self-Reflection)

Monday

How do you balance the need for rest and the call to action? Do you practice Sabbath regularly?

Tuesday

Reflect on the following paragraph and the subsequent prayer, based on Psalm 46:10. After each line from the psalm, take a breath and reflect on the words before you move to the next line. How does each line of diminished words shift in meaning? How does this lead you to experience the psalm in a new way?

The God who causes the heart to rest after every single beat. The God who calls the sun to set every day with no exception. The God who makes the ocean tide go out, lungs to exhale, animals to hibernate, and leaves to change and fall to the ground. This is the same God who invites each of us to lean into the sacredness of rest.

> Be still and know that I am God.
> Be still and know that I am.
> Be still and know.
> Be still.
> Be.[18]

Wednesday

Take a moment today to read slowly and intentionally through this week's passage, Exodus 16:2–30. What do you find compelling about this story? What stands out to you most strongly and why?

Thursday

What area of your life currently feels like day 2? What do you feel that you need in this situation in order to persevere? How can you ask God for these things while looking around you to see where God may already by providing for you—through your support system or by prompting you to rest?

Friday

Reflect on the quote by Sonya Renee Taylor at the end of the chapter. What "stitching skills" have you learned in your own wilderness experiences? How might they help you move forward?

Saturday

Practice Sabbath rest today or tomorrow. What does "gathering manna" usually look like for you? Do not gather manna today.

Sharing Together

(Group Discussion Questions)

1. How do you find a routine of rest in your busy life? How do you celebrate Sabbath? And if you haven't been able to celebrate and honor Sabbath, where might there be an invitation, however small, to do so?
2. Share aspects of your life or the life of your religious community that currently feel like day 2.
3. What specific things in your life make it difficult to rest?

Taking Action

(Next Steps)

1. Do you need to take action by resting? Perhaps follow the example of the Nap Ministry and find out more about practicing rest as resistance. Learn more about Tricia Hersey's work by reading her book *Rest Is Resistance: A Manifesto* (New York: Little, Brown Spark, 2022).
2. Consider whether you feel called to step further into the work of justice and allow someone else who has been active in the work the time to rest. Where do you see opportunities to do this?

3. This week's action recommendations concern rest and Sabbath because we all need to take time away from work, even the work of justice. As you enjoy a true Sabbath day this week, think about how you can continue a regular practice of unplugging and decompressing. Can you make an intention not to check work email or to put any extra activities on your schedule one day every week, or every other week?

The Next Right Thing

Exodus 17:1–7

Joy in the Face of Despair

I (Mary Alice) shared earlier in this book about my friend Brenda who passed away from pancreatic cancer. Before her diagnosis, Brenda had been experiencing some stomach pain; doctors discovered she had a large mass on her pancreas. She was rushed into emergency surgery in Dallas only to learn that the cancer had already spread too far. Doctors explained that they had done everything possible and that Brenda had only months to live.

I remember driving home after her surgery, absolutely heartbroken. I still needed to write a sermon for our church's annual Palm Sunday worship service in the park that weekend, a celebratory event complete with children waving palm branches, a picnic, and a community Easter egg hunt. Nothing in me felt like celebrating that day when I was living in the devastation of Good Friday. I did not want to get out of bed, let alone preach a sermon. However, that was when I began to hear the message Jesus gives us on Palm Sunday in a way I never had before.

For us, Palm Sunday is a day of celebration as the journey of Lent moves us toward Holy Week. On that first Palm Sunday, Jesus knows, all too well, what is ahead of him. Jesus knows that his death is imminent. He knows that some of the people praising him in these moments and shouting "Hosanna!" from the streets will turn their backs on him just days later. Jesus has every reason to tell the disciples, "You all need to quiet down. Things are about to get bad for me, and we don't need to make matters worse. Let's just go quietly into Jerusalem—after all, this is more of a funeral procession for me than it is a celebratory parade. The party's over, everybody."

However, this isn't at all what we see happen. In the face of death, Jesus knows he cannot play it safe. He cannot give in to weariness or defeat. Perhaps the message Jesus gives us on Palm Sunday is to be brave, foolish, and risky enough to live boldly, even in the face of despair. To clap our hands! To raise our voices! To celebrate in the streets, even when we know death is just around the corner.

Jesus embodies what theologian Willie Jennings reminds us, that joy can be "an act of resistance against the forces of death and despair."[1] Jesus soaks in every last bit of this Palm Sunday parade in defiance of the Roman Empire. He invites us to do the same; even when death and despair may be around the corner, joy is something that cannot be taken away from us.

I think of my friend Brenda every year on Palm Sunday. She, too, knew joy was an act of resistance against the diagnosis she had received, and she dared to live out this audacious message, even in the last days of her life.

Like Brenda and the disciples, Jesus invites us into a space of joyful resistance, even when it feels as if the world is falling apart around us. During Holy Week, we are invited to be brave enough to trust in God, even when it feels risky and the world tells us to quiet down and play it safe. We are called to keep doing the next right thing with each moment we are entrusted and to keep taking brave steps forward.

Thirsty without Water (Exod. 17:1–7)

The Israelites' world seems to continue falling apart as they make their way through the wilderness. In Exodus 17, they arrive at Rephidim, a place without water. The people are thirsty and begin crying out for something to drink. The story does not indicate how many days the Israelites were without water, but one hundred hours is often cited as the length of time a person without a source of water can survive at average temperatures. That is a little over four days. According to Anathea Portier-Young, Old Testament professor at Duke Divinity School, in today's Sinai Peninsula, the average high temperatures are 95 degrees Fahrenheit in May and 104 in June. "In such extreme heat and with exposure to sun, the timeline for survival shortens considerably."[2]

Their thirst, therefore, is not a petty complaint or a light matter. Water is a serious issue for those weary, hot travelers. Finding themselves at a place lacking water, people begin to cry out and question God. They consider what good their trip out of Egypt might hold if they are only going to die of thirst in the midst of a dry desert. They start wondering about God's presence among them. In Exodus 17:7, they ask pointedly, "Is the LORD among us or not?"

If God Is with Us . . .

Notice how quickly the Israelites fall back into their former way of dualistic, win/lose, either-or thinking, asking why Moses brought them out of slavery in the first place: "Is God among us, leading us forward, or not? And if God is with us, then why is there no water?" We can critique the Israelites, but we do well to acknowledge the raw honesty of their question, a question we would likely ask if we were in their situation. Indeed, many of us have asked a version of "is God among us?" in the midst of our own experiences of pain and injustice:

If God is with us, why does our world seem to be falling apart right now?
If God is with us, why do I struggle with this addiction, illness, or disability?
If God is with us, why is the system stacked against me? Or against other marginalized communities?
If God is with us, why did I lose my loved one far too soon?

We can be tempted to fit our theology into these constraints of human logic. If X happens, then Y is not supposed to happen. If God is with us, then a lengthy list of things are simply not supposed to happen. They do not fit into our "God equation." On our own, we cannot reconcile how both could plausibly be true at the same time; it has to be one or the other to fit into the neat and tidy boxes of X and Y. Consequently, when Y does happen, the logical response is to reexamine X and to ask the same question the Israelites ask in the wilderness, "Is the LORD among us or not?"

But notice that it is Moses, not God, who is losing patience and is upset by the Israelites' questions. As we have written previously, God is familiar with the language of protest and lament—the raw vulnerability of God's people crying out for what they need. In this instance, it is Moses, not God, who is upset by the people's protest in the wilderness! When Moses brings the situation to God, he still doesn't seem concerned for the people's well-being or where they are going to get something to drink. He doesn't even ask God where water could be found for his people. Instead, afraid the people are going to kill him, he asks God what he should do about them.

Moses is more concerned about the people's *protesting* than *why* they are upset in the first place. He does not seem to want to find a solution to their problem in the wilderness but wants to keep them calm and under control. Does that sound familiar when you consider responses to modern-day protests for liberation like those against police brutality toward our Black and brown communities? We have seen people more concerned about the methods of protesting than the injustices the protests represent. Many people are tempted to be more upset about destroyed property than destroyed lives, as the Rev. Ron Bell pointed out in the wake of George Floyd's murder (see p. 49). In a 1967 speech at Stanford University, Martin Luther King Jr. declared, "In the final analysis, a riot is the language of the unheard. And what is it that America has failed to hear?"[3] He was not condoning riots in this speech but viewing them as a symptom of a people who are not heard. It may take effort to redirect our attention to the pain and suffering in others' lives as we seek to understand why people are marching in the streets. Why are they protesting?

God is paying attention to the "why," to the need that motivates the Israelites' protest. In Exodus 17:5 God tells Moses what to do next: get water for the people in the wilderness. Valerie Bridgeman, a biblical scholar and professor at the Methodist Theological School of Ohio, paraphrases this story: "God says to Moses, 'Grab some of the elders to go with you. Come on, let's go. You've seen this before. Take that staff. The thing that's already in your hand. The one that you used at sea last time. Now go forward with that. And look ahead, because I'll be standing there. I'll be right in front of you. Strike the rock with the stick, and the people will have water to drink.'"[4]

God reveals to Moses the next right thing to do. God reminds Moses of the resources around him and encourages him to use them in this moment. In the midst of a completely overwhelming situation, there is water in the wilderness; in a location lacking water, in the middle of the desert, and out of a rock, there is water freely flowing. The people of God are not out of the wilderness yet, but they have what they need to make it through another day, their lives sustained in their life-threatening environment.

The Next Right Thing

In her book *The Next Right Thing*, Emily Freeman says that Jesus frequently instructs people in Scripture by showing them a small step to take next. For instance, when Jesus performs a miracle, she says, he often gives people a simple next thing to do. He tells the leper to tell no one about what has happened, but to go and show himself to the priest (Matt. 8:4). To the person with paralysis, he says to get up, take his bed, and go home (Matt. 9:1–8; Mark 2:1–12; Luke 5:17–26; John 5:5–9). After raising Jairus's daughter from the dead, he instructs Jairus and his wife to give her something to eat (Mark 5:21–43). "At first glance, that seems like a waste of a captive audience," Freeman says. "Rather than a life plan, a clear vision, or a five-year list of goals, the leper, the paralytic, and Jairus and his wife were given clear instructions by Jesus about what to do next—and only *next*."[5]

It's important for us to note that, more often than not, the next right thing is not monumental or extraordinary. It is not ending systemic racism or bringing down the patriarchy or solving generational poverty. Those lofty and laudable goals are too big and complex for a single step. The next right thing is manageable and within reach. The next right thing invites us to take a realistic step and to trust God will lead us as we take the next one and the one after that. For some of us, this next step may feel huge, and for others, it may feel like it's not enough. Perhaps the next right thing is the "daily bread" or the water in the wilderness we ask God to provide—not bread for a week or a month or a lifetime, but for "this day."

Friends who are part of the recovery community have shared with us how this concept is common within the language of addiction recovery as well. The focus in recovery is not on tomorrow's sobriety but on today's. The idea actually originated with psychiatrist Carl Jung, who advised a patient that even though she did not know the future, she did know the "next and most necessary thing" to do. Sometimes, when we focus on the end goal, it feels overwhelming and completely out of reach, so we do not even bother to take the first step. The challenge immobilizes us. But when we shift our focus and attention to the present moment, to the next and most necessary thing, we are equipped to keep moving forward toward our end goal.

God showed the people the next right thing to do to live another day in the wilderness. God met their immediate need of water; God did not immediately rescue them from the wilderness.

King's Kitchen Table

We often look to Martin Luther King Jr. for the many ways he helped to bring lasting, systemic change during the Civil Rights Movement. However, we do not get many glimpses of the smaller, day-to-day actions and decisions he made that contributed to his transformative work.

One of the biggest turning points in King's journey happened at his own kitchen table late one Friday night, January 27, 1956. He and his family had moved to Montgomery in 1954 for him to become the pastor of Dexter Avenue Baptist Church. He actually had no intention of becoming involved in the Civil Rights protests until the Montgomery bus boycott, which began in early December 1955 after Rosa Parks's refusal to give up her bus seat to a white man. King was asked to become president of the Montgomery Improvement Association, the pastors' group leading the boycott. When he accepted, he thought surely they could resolve this issue fairly quickly. However, nearly two months later, tensions were still escalating, and it felt as if they were getting nowhere. He had already been in jail once at this point (for driving thirty miles per hour in a twenty-five-miles-per-hour zone). He had submitted his resignation letter to the association, but none of them would accept it.

King came home late one night after another strategy meeting only to answer yet another horrific phone call from an unknown caller using vulgar words against him and threatening to kill his family. At first, King had tried to brush off the threatening calls and letters, but now he was getting thirty to forty a day, and they were only getting worse. King hung up the phone, walked to the kitchen, put on a pot of coffee with trembling hands, and sank into a chair at his kitchen table. Writing of this experience, he said:

> I was ready to give up. With my cup of coffee sitting untouched before me, I tried to think of a way to move out of the picture without appearing a coward. In this state of exhaustion, when my courage had all but gone, I decided to take my problem to God. With my head in my hands, I bowed over the kitchen table and prayed aloud. The words I spoke to God that midnight are still vivid in my memory. "I am here taking a stand for what I believe is right. But now I am afraid. The people are looking to me for leadership, and if I stand before them without strength and courage, they too will falter. I am at the end of my powers. I have nothing left. I've come to the point where I can't face it alone."
>
> At that moment, I experienced the presence of the Divine as I had never experienced [God] before. It seemed as though I could hear the quiet assurance of an inner voice saying: "Stand up for righteousness, stand up for truth; and God will be at your side forever." Almost at once my fears began to go. My uncertainty disappeared. I was ready to face anything.[6]

That experience at the kitchen table gave King the courage to keep doing what felt like the next right thing. He continued pastoring and investing himself in the Montgomery Improvement Association. Three days later, King's house was bombed while his family was inside, and they barely escaped. He said it was his kitchen table epiphany which sustained and carried him through. He would go on to lead the Civil Rights effort until his death in 1968, twelve years later. To this day, people tour the Kings' parsonage in Montgomery, Alabama, often asking if they can sit at the kitchen table where King had his epiphany. The coffee cups the family used are still in place.

We know the rest of King's story. His actions, the next right things for him, led to the founding of the Southern Christian Leadership Conference (SCLC) in 1957, the March on Washington in 1963, the Civil Rights Act of 1964, and the marches in Selma and Voting Rights Act of 1965. We also know that doing the next right thing ultimately led to King's death in 1968 when he was assassinated while he was standing on the second-floor balcony outside his hotel room in Memphis, Tennessee. He was in Memphis to help lead a protest on behalf of the striking Memphis sanitation workers, the next right thing for him. King's life is a reminder that doing the next right thing is never insignificant or inconsequential. It is as revolutionary as it is risky.

Holy Saturday: The Space between Good Friday and Easter Sunday

Most of our lives are lived in the space between the painful and unjust realities of this world and the hope of liberation and new life. We live between "O sacred Head, now wounded, with grief and shame weighed down"[7] and "Love's redeeming work is done! Alleluia!"[8] Most of life happens in this liminal space between Good Friday and Easter Sunday. The space between despair and hope, death and resurrection, in the messy middle.

And yet, consider what happens in the devastating hours after Jesus' death and before the resurrection. Joseph of Arimathea takes the body of Jesus from the cross and places it in the tomb. Did he understand the risk he was taking in doing this? Romans normally did not allow executed persons to be taken by their supporters. And Joseph was not just any supporter; he was a "good and righteous man . . . who, though a member of the council, had not agreed to their plan and action" (Luke 23:50–51a).

Luke describes Joseph as a man "waiting expectantly for the kingdom of God" (23:51b). This phrase is often used to describe faithful

Jews (Simeon and Anna are described this way in Luke 2:25, 36–38). It distinguishes Joseph as a respectable person, yet his actions do not suggest he is only "waiting expectantly" for something big and exciting to happen. He is doing the next right thing he can do, the mundane work he knows needs to be done.

Notice how the author of Luke pays careful attention to Joseph's actions: he *went* to Pilate, *asked* for the body of Jesus, *took* the body, *wrapped* the body, *laid* the body. Likewise, the women who come with Joseph are characterized by their actions: they *came* from Galilee, *followed* Joseph, *saw* the tomb, *returned* home, and *prepared* the spices (23:52–56). All of these are simple, ordinary actions. Some require getting a little dirty, going out of one's way, or being uncomfortable, but these sorts of actions would never be recognized or praised by others as being significant in any way. In fact, there are probably far more urgent things Joseph and these women could have been doing. Yet they came. They asked. They followed. They wrapped. They returned. They prepared. These were small and seemingly insignificant actions, yet they were done with great care and tremendous love for Jesus.

In his book *The Irresistible Revolution,* Shane Claiborne writes about the time he spent in Calcutta at the Home for the Destitute and Dying, which had been started by Mother Teresa. He writes,

> I helped folks eat, massaged muscles, gave baths, and basically tried to spoil people who really deserved it. Each day, folks would die, and each day, we would go out onto the streets and bring in new people. The goal was not to keep people alive (we had very few supplies for doing that) but to allow people to die with dignity, with someone loving them, singing, laughing, so they were not alone. Sometimes folks with medical training would come by and be overwhelmed with frustration because we had so few medical supplies, and the sisters would hastily explain that our mission was not to prolong life but to help people die well . . . .
>
> While the temptation to do great things is always before us, in Khalighat I learned the discipline of doing small things with great deliberation. Mother Teresa used to say, "We can do no great things, just small things with great love."[9]

Joseph and the women did not do anything great or remarkable, simply small things with great love for Jesus. On their day 2, they faithfully did the next right thing. When we approach the work of justice and love in this way, doing the smallest tasks of ministry with the greatest love for Jesus, perhaps then we get a glimpse of what the kin-dom of God really looks like.

In the story of Joseph and the women at the tomb, we see a hopeless situation but also a beautiful picture of the kin-dom of God breaking into the world. Preacher and professor Fred Craddock notes Jesus is "honored, symbolically speaking, by the entire country. . . . The women of Galilee . . . . Joseph [from Judea] . . . . [People from] north and south Palestine, male and female join to tell the reader that for all that has occurred Jesus has not been totally abandoned."[10] Luke makes a place in this story for hope, even in a seemingly hopeless situation, giving the reader reason to believe the story has not yet ended.

We, too, know the story has not yet ended. When there seems to be no hope, we are reminded that this kin-dom Jesus came to bring about has not been totally abandoned. As with Joseph and the women at the tomb, we are called to do our part. In our journey from awakening to action, we are invited to keep doing the next right thing.

The Spiritual Awakening at Asbury University

In February 2023, a couple dozen students at Asbury University in Wilmore, Kentucky (about an hour away from us in Louisville), stayed after a weekly chapel service on campus and continued worshiping and praying together. The word about their continued worship gathering began to spread across campus, and other students began to join in throughout the day. By the evening, some students were seen dragging mattresses into the chapel to spend the night in this sacred space of spontaneous worship.

For the following two weeks, word about what was happening at Asbury continued to spread through both social media and word of mouth. What's fascinating is that this worship wasn't loud or showy;

there were no long evangelistic sermons, flashing lights, or smoke machines. It appeared homegrown, led by various groups of people praying, singing, and simply worshiping together. And people continued to come. Tens of thousands of people from college campuses and churches across the country began to pour into the small chapel. Overflow locations were set up across campus and a large screen livestreaming the service was set up on the campus lawn. People would stand in line for hours to get a short glimpse of what was happening in the chapel. The university estimates that it drew more than fifty thousand people to the town of Wilmore, whose population is merely six thousand people.

Our hope throughout this Lenten study has been to show how moments of spiritual awakening always ought to lead us toward some kind of action; holy experiences ought to have holy consequences in the world around us. As we complete the writing of this book, the question remains, what will be the result of the awakening at Asbury?

The reality is that prior moments of spiritual awakening in our country haven't led to much social transformation. The First Great Awakening that spread through the New England colonies between the 1730s and 1770s was a revival of religious fervor, and the Second Great Awakening from 1795 to 1835 was filled with camp meetings that spread that same religious fervor across the country, and yet these awakenings were taking place at the height of the spread of slavery, a sin that continues to haunt our country and seep into our soiled systems of inequity to this day. The jury is still out as to whether this most recent awakening at Asbury will be different.

The questions we can hope to answer together as our Lenten journey comes to an end are more personal: Where will your moments of spiritual awakening lead you? And what will be your next right thing?

Sticky Notes of Courage

I (Mary Alice) have a box of cards, notes, and mementos people have given me over the years that I often look through whenever I am having a hard day and need encouragement. I was going through that box recently, and at the top was a sticky note a friend sent me a few years ago. I had been sharing with her about a significant decision I needed to make, and I did not know if I had it in me—if I was ready to take the next step. A few days later, she mailed a card with this small yellow sticky note inside that said just the words I needed in that moment: "You can do this. You have everything you need." I kept it on my refrigerator for the following year as a reminder that I had everything I needed to do what God was calling me to do. And on the days when I wasn't sure if I believed it, I went to see my friend's handwriting on my refrigerator door. Because if she believed this about me, then maybe I could believe it for myself, too.

What do you need for the next brave step God is calling you toward? If we stop for a moment and pay attention, we may find that the resources we need are already all around us: in the people who journey with us, those who believe in us when we can't believe in ourselves; in all that God has gifted and entrusted to us; and in the modern-day staffs God has placed in our hands. Sometimes, we even see God with us in the words of a friend scribbled on a sticky note and stuck on our refrigerator door.

When Moses turned aside at the burning bush, his moment of spiritual awakening led him to help liberate the Hebrew people from slavery. In the wilderness, the Israelites received continued messages of God's sustaining presence with them. Still, they first had to take the next brave step into the waters. They were given a pillar of cloud by day and fire by night to guide them. They gathered manna and quail in the wilderness, but they had to have the courage to strike the rock to discover flowing water. Each time they were reminded of the Holy One's presence with them, they had a step to take, a job to do, and a way to be part of God's continued work along the journey. The same is true for us today in the midst of our real wilderness moments.

As you complete this book and approach the season of Easter, we aren't even close to arriving in the promised land of justice and equity for all our siblings in all our diverse identities and backgrounds. The wilderness surrounding us remains daunting and overwhelming. However, we have everything we need for this hard and holy work ahead of us. The question is, what will be our brave next step?

Lenten Practices

Paying Attention

(Self-Reflection)

Monday

Consider the next right action for you to take as a response to this Lenten study.

What do you need for the next brave step God is calling you to take? Do you believe you have what you need to make it through the messy middle?

Tuesday

Reflect on this question: If God is with us, why does the world seem to be falling apart right now? How might we reframe this question to consider God's presence among us?

Wednesday

Slowly and intentionally read this week's Scripture passage, Exodus 17:1–7. What do you find compelling about this story? Where do the words draw you in, sparking a thought or feeling?

Maundy Thursday

On this day, we remember Jesus' last supper with his disciples. What might it look like for you to create a welcome table for others, in your home, in your place of work, in your church?

Good Friday

What crucifying situations do you see around you? Who do you see suffering and in pain?

Holy Saturday

Read Luke 23:50–56 and consider the space between Good Friday and Easter Sunday. What elements in this passage and the experience of being suspended between death and life resonate with your own experience of working for justice?

Sharing Together
(Group Discussion Questions)

1. Discuss some possible "next right things"—actions your group might take at the end of this Lenten study.

2. Share your experience of Holy Week. How does Holy Week feel different in light of this study? What new lens do you bring to this spiritual journey through the last days before Jesus' crucifixion?

3. Sometimes when we feel overwhelmed, we think we have nothing to offer in the face of significant challenges. To respond to this feeling, take a moment to create some lists of your skills, resources, and contacts (both individually and as a group). What can you bring practically to a demanding situation? How does making these lists make you feel—about yourself or about God?

4. As you complete this study, reflect on the phrase "hard and holy work." How do you see the call to spiritual awakening and social action as both challenging and lifegiving work?

Taking Action
(Next Steps)

1. Do the next right thing this week. Take that step.

2. If God were to mail you a sticky note of courage for this upcoming season of life, what would its message be? Reflect on what your sticky note might say, and write it out. Then place it on your refrigerator, bathroom mirror, or somewhere you will see it often as a word of hope for the season ahead.

3. Make a list of some more ideas for possible "next right things"—concrete, doable, small actions you plan to take during this Easter season to celebrate resurrection and liberation. Take some regular time of prayer and discernment in the coming weeks to continue to determine what particular steps you feel called to keep taking toward God's vision of justice.

Small-Group Study Guide

Lent invites us to explore the faithful intersections of spiritual awakening and social action. One important avenue for this exploration is through small-group interactions. These groups allow us to discuss our faith journeys as they relate to the material in this book. In a small group, we hear from others how God is present in their lives, and how God calls us to action individually and in community.

This study is organized so that each book chapter corresponds to a week in the Lenten season. We therefore recommend a weekly meeting of the group to discuss the material. If you meet for the first time during the week of Ash Wednesday, then you will have seven sessions before Easter Sunday.

Session 1: Beginning the Journey of Lent	Ash Wednesday
Session 2: Not on My Watch	First Week of Lent
Session 3: Paying Attention, Seeing Injustice	Second Week of Lent
Session 4: Look Again!	Third Week of Lent
Session 5: Wade in the Water	Fourth Week of Lent
Session 6: Finding God on Day 2	Fifth Week of Lent
Session 7: The Next Right Thing	Holy Week

At the conclusion of each book chapter, we invite you to reflect, engage, and respond to what you have read through different types of activities. All of these activities would be appropriate to discuss in a small-group setting as you ponder together how this Lenten season and the book of Exodus continue to speak today. Free videos for each session of the study are also available at https://tinyurl.com/WJKYouTube. These short videos of us introducing each chapter are ideal to help provide your group with a starting point to engage with and discuss the book. You can use the videos to begin group sessions or as an introduction for each participant to watch beforehand.

Daily questions in the **Paying Attention** section are meant primarily for individual reflection. However, these could also be used as discussion questions for a group. Your group can decide how you want to handle these questions. Perhaps group members want to use these reflections daily for their private reflection time. Or perhaps a leader or selected group member can choose one of these daily reflections to bring to the group each week.

The **Sharing Together** section was designed to be used in small groups and provides questions to engage in the week's reading. You may want to center these questions during your small-group discussion. A leader may want to guide the group through them as the main priority for each session.

The final section at the end of each chapter is **Taking Action** activities. This section provides concrete opportunities to engage in your community. In a group setting, you may decide to use this section to respond to the study's materials as a group. Or you may want to discuss how you might respond individually to some of the suggestions.

Acknowledgments

I (Mary Alice) am especially grateful to my cowriter, Tyler, who first imagined the idea of creating this hard and holy work together. You have been a dear friend and trusted guide throughout the writing process, and I'm so glad to have shared this sacred space with you. Thanks also to my beloved faith communities at Highland Baptist Church of Louisville, Kentucky, and Calvary Baptist Church in Waco, Texas, whose faithful work and prophetic witness inspired this book. We started writing shortly after I left Calvary and not long after I arrived at Highland during the COVID-19 pandemic. This creative process challenged me to find and to trust my voice in the midst of an ever-changing world. Lastly, thanks to my husband, Evan Jacoby, for his faithful support through this journey, particularly when I realized I would be submitting this book just days before our wedding! Thank you for being a constant encourager and grounding presence of love in my life.

I (Tyler) am grateful to participate in the supportive communities of Louisville Presbyterian Theological Seminary, St. Andrew United Church of Christ, and Highland Baptist Church. You all provide hope and vision for my work as a theological educator. Many thanks to my wonderful family—Lauren, Livia, Jude, and Taft—for all the laughs and for loving me for who I am and not what I do. And thanks especially to Mary Alice, who agreed to create this study with me. I'm thankful for your ministry!

We both are thankful for many friends and colleagues who read this book and offered helpful comments: Cinda King, Heather McIntyre, Todd Smith, Devin Pettiford, Elana Keppel Levy, Beth Olker, Ashley Drake Mertz, Daniel Van Beek, Teresa Larson, Lauren Jones Mayfield, Jon Singletary, and Angela Gorrell. In addition, Julie Mullins and Julie Tonini, our thoughtful editors at WJK, provided wonderful support during this project.

Notes

Ash Wednesday

1. Thomas Merton, *Conjectures of a Guilty Bystander* (New York: Doubleday, 1966), 140–42.
2. Michael Washburn, "Exploring Louisville's Enchanting, Peculiar Thomas Merton Marker," Louisville Public Media, April 1, 2016, https://wfpl.org/exploring-thomas-merton-epiphany-marker-louisville/.
3. Washburn, "Louisville's Thomas Merton Marker."
4. Tessa Duvall and Hayes Gardner, "'You Need to Be Reminded of Breonna': How a Tiny City Park Became the Heart of a Movement," *Louisville Courier Journal*, last updated March 13, 2022, https://www.courier-journal.com/in-depth/news/local/breonna-taylor/2021/03/04/why-jefferson-square-park-important-to-breonna-taylor-protesters/6771061002/.
5. Ijeoma Oluo, *So You Want to Talk About Race* (New York: Seal Press, 2019), 66.
6. For more information regarding the Slave Bible, see Michael Martin's interview of Anthony Schmidt, "Slave Bible from the 1800s Omitted Key Passages That Could Incite Rebellion," *All Things Considered*, NPR, December 9, 2018, https://www.npr.org/transcripts/674995075.
7. Andrew Prevot, "The Hope of Exodus in Black Theology," Lumen Christi Institute's Black Catholic Initiative, May 9, 2019, http://lumenchristi.org/event/2019/05/hope-of-exodus-in-black-womanist-theology-andrew-prevot.
8. Anne Lamott, *Plan B: Further Thoughts on Faith* (New York: Penguin, 2006), 257.
9. Cole Arthur Riley, *This Here Flesh: Spirituality, Liberation, and the Stories That Make Us* (New York: Convergent, 2022), x.

The First Week of Lent

1. Greta Gerwig, shooting script for *Lady Bird,* directed by Greta Gerwig (2017), available at Daily Script, https://www.dailyscript.com/scripts/LADY_BIRD_shooting_script.pdf.
2. Nadia Bolz-Weber, *Shameless: A Case for Not Feeling Bad for Feeling Good (about Sex)* (New York: Convergent, 2019), 90.
3. Wilda C. Gafney, *Womanist Midrash: A Reintroduction to the Women of the Torah and the Throne* (Louisville, KY: Westminster John Knox Press, 2017), 91.
4. "Jodie Foster's Golden Globes Speech: Full Transcript," ABC News, January 14, 2013, https://abcnews.go.com/blogs/entertainment/2013/01/full-transcript-jodie-fosters-golden-globes-speech.
5. Kathryn Freeman, "Voices: Breonna Taylor, Invisible Black Women and God Who Sees Us," *Baptist Standard,* May 20, 2020, https://www.baptiststandard.com/opinion/voices/breonna-taylor-invisible-black-women-god-who-sees-us/.
6. Kirsten Weir, "Inequality at School: What's Behind the Racial Disparity in Our Education System?," *Monitor on Psychology* 47, no. 10 (November 2016), https://www.apa.org/monitor/2016/11/cover-inequality-school.
7. Ashley Nellis, "Mass Incarceration Trends," Sentencing Project, January 25, 2023, https://www.sentencingproject.org/reports/mass-incarceration-trends/.
8. "History of Hymns: 'His Eye Is on the Sparrow,'" Discipleship Ministries, United Methodist Church, June 25, 2013, https://www.umcdiscipleship.org/resources/history-of-hymns-his-eye-is-on-the-sparrow.
9. Civilla Durfee Martin, "Why Should I Feel Discouraged? (His Eye Is on the Sparrow)," *Glory to God* (Louisville, KY: Westminster John Knox Press, 2013), 661.
10. Wil Gafney, "Black and Christian: An MLK Day Sermon," January 17, 2016, https://www.wilgafney.com/2016/01/17/black-and-christian-an-mlk-day-sermon/.
11. Ijeoma Oluo, *So You Want to Talk About Race* (New York: Seal Press, 2019), 65.

The Second Week of Lent

1. *National Geographic,* "A Double Dutch," *Brain Games,* January 27, 2014, https://youtu.be/iiEzf3J4iFk.
2. Daniel Simons, "But Did You See the Gorilla? The Problem with Inattentional Blindness," *Smithsonian Magazine,* September 2012, https://www.smithsonianmag.com/science-nature/but-did-you-see-the-gorilla-the-problem-with-inattentional-blindness-17339778/.
3. Terence E. Fretheim, *Exodus,* Interpretation (Louisville, KY: Westminster John Knox Press, 1991), 42–43.
4. Dr. Seuss, *Horton Hears a Who!* (New York: Random House, 1954).
5. Learn more about Kara Ayers and her consulting firm called Mind Ramps at https://mindramps.com. Kara and her husband, Adam, started this organization to envision "a diverse, equitable, inclusive and disabled future."

6. Public Religion Research Institute, "American Bubbles: Politics, Race, and Religion in Americans' Core Friendship Networks," May 24, 2022, https://www.prri.org/research/american-bubbles-politics-race-and-religion-in-americans-core-friendship-networks/.
7. Christopher Ingraham, "Three Quarters of Whites Don't Have Any Non-white Friends," *Washington Post,* August 25, 2014, https://www.washingtonpost.com/news/wonk/wp/2014/08/25/three-quarters-of-whites-dont-have-any-non-white-friends/.
8. Kelly Brown Douglas, *Resurrection Hope: A Future Where Black Lives Matter* (Maryknoll, NY: Orbis, 2021), 163.
9. Fannie Lou Hamer, from a 1971 speech, in *The Speeches of Fannie Lou Hamer: To Tell It Like It Is,* ed. Maegan Parker Brooks and Davis W. Houck (Jackson: University Press of Mississippi, 2011), 125.
10. *13th,* directed by Ava DuVernay (2016); *Crip Camp: A Disability Revolution,* directed by Nicole Newnham and Jim LeBrecht (2020); Bryan Stevenson, *Just Mercy: A Story of Justice and Redemption* (New York: Spiegel & Grau, 2014); Kiese Laymon, *Heavy: An American Memoir* (New York: Scribner, 2018).

The Third Week of Lent

1. Gene Weingarten, "Pearls before Breakfast: Can One of the Nation's Great Musicians Cut Through the Fog of a D.C. Rush Hour? Let's Find Out," *Washington Post,* April 8, 2007.
2. Terence E. Fretheim, *Exodus,* Interpretation (Louisville, KY: Westminster John Knox Press, 1991), 53–54.
3. Randall Bradley wrote regularly throughout his wife Brenda's journey with cancer and since her death. If you're interested in reading more, visit https://www.caringbridge.org/visit/brendabradley2.
4. Marilynne Robinson, *Gilead* (New York: Farrar, Straus & Giroux, 2004), 245.
5. Richard Rohr, "Liberation Theology," Center for Action and Contemplation, March 20, 2016, https://cac.org/liberation-theology-2016-03-20/.
6. Ron Bell, "Do Not Look Away!," blog post, May 29, 2020, https://www.drronbell.com/post/do-not-look-away.
7. Elizabeth Barrett Browning, *Aurora Leigh*, 2nd ed. (London: Chapman and Hall, 1857), 304.
8. Chris Palmer, "How to Overcome Impostor Phenomenon," *Monitor on Psychology* 52, no. 4 (June 2021), https://www.apa.org/monitor/2021/06/cover-impostor-phenomenon.
9. Michael Calia, "Watch Natalie Portman's Frank, Personal Harvard Commencement Speech," *Wall Street Journal,* May 28, 2015, https://www.wsj.com/articles/BL-SEB-89051.
10. Josh Jones, "John Steinbeck Has a Crisis in Confidence while Writing *The Grapes of Wrath,*" *Open Culture,* July 12, 2017, https://www.openculture.com

/2017/07/john-steinbeck-has-a-crisis-in-confidence-while-writing-the-grapes-of-wrath.html.

11. Sheryl Sandberg, *Lean In: Women, Work, and the Will to Lead* (New York: Alfred A. Knopf, 2013), 28.
12. Kathy Khang, *Raise Your Voice: Why We Stay Silent and How to Speak Up* (Downers Grove, IL: InterVarsity Press, 2018), 33.
13. "What Is Mindfulness? The Founder of Mindfulness-Based Stress Reduction Explains," *Mindful*, January 11, 2017, https://www.mindful.org/jon-kabat-zinn-defining-mindfulness/.

The Fourth Week of Lent

1. Richard Rohr, "An Economy of Grace," Center for Action and Contemplation, May 23, 2017, https://cac.org/daily-meditations/an-economy-of-grace-2017-05-23/.
2. Elizabeth Gilbert, *Big Magic: Creative Living beyond Fear* (New York: Riverhead Books, 2015), 25.
3. Gilbert, *Big Magic,* 25–26.
4. Gilbert, *Big Magic,* 26.
5. Peter L. Steinke, *Uproar: Calm Leadership in Anxious Times* (Lanham, MD: Rowman & Littlefield, 2019), 40.
6. Anne Lamott, "12 Truths I Learned from Life and Writing," TED2017, https://www.ted.com/talks/anne_lamott_12_truths_i_learned_from_life_and_writing.
7. Dr. Martin Luther King Jr., "Remaining Awake through a Great Revolution" (sermon at the National Cathedral in Washington, DC, March 31, 1968), in *A Testament of Hope: The Essential Writings of Martin Luther King, Jr.*, ed. James Melvin Washington (San Francisco: Harper & Row, 1986), 277.
8. Terence E. Fretheim, *Exodus,* Interpretation (Louisville, KY: Westminster John Knox Press, 1991), 159.
9. Brian McLaren, *The Great Spiritual Migration: How the World's Largest Religion Is Seeking a Better Way to Be Christian* (New York: Convergent Books, 2016), 203.
10. John Kohan, "*Exodus: Journeys of Liberation*, by Carl Dixon," *Christian Century,* September 11, 2019, https://www.christiancentury.org/article/art/exodus-journeys-liberation-carl-dixon; "Carl Dixon," Sacred Art Pilgrim,_http://sacredartpilgrim.com/collection/view/50.
11. Joel Gunter, "Harriet Tubman: Former Slave Who Risked All to Save Others," *BBC News,* April 21, 2016, https://www.bbc.com/news/business-36099791.
12. History.com editors, "Harriet Tubman," History, updated March 29, 2023, https://www.history.com/topics/black-history/harriet-tubman.
13. Kate Clifford Larson, *Harriet Tubman: A Reference Guide to Her Life and Works* (Lanham, MD: Rowman and Littlefield, 2022), 165.
14. John Lewis, tweet from June 2018, quoted in Joshua Bote, "'Get in Good Trouble, Necessary Trouble': Rep. John Lewis in His Own Words," *USA Today,*

updated July 19, 2020, https://www.usatoday.com/story/news/politics/2020/07/18/rep-john-lewis-most-memorable-quotes-get-good-trouble/5464148002/.

15. Rabbi Stephanie Kolin as quoted in McLaren, *Great Spiritual Migration*, 202.

The Fifth Week of Lent

1. Brené Brown, *Rising Strong: How the Ability to Reset Transforms the Way We Live, Love, Parent, and Lead* (New York: Random House, 2017), 12.
2. Brown, *Rising Strong*, 26–27.
3. Elna Solvang, "Commentary on Exodus 16:2–4, 9–15," Working Preacher, August 2, 2009, https://www.workingpreacher.org/commentaries/revised-common-lectionary/ordinary-18-2/commentary-on-exodus-162-4-9-15-2.
4. Mary Alice Birdwhistell and Lauren Jones Mayfield, "At Christmas, Jesus Bears the Light of Justice. We Need It More Than Ever," *Louisville Courier Journal*, December 18, 2020, https://www.courier-journal.com/story/opinion/2020/12/18/louisville-needs-find-light-justice-after-160-homicides-2022/6548541002/.
5. "Science: Manna," *Time*, August 29, 1927, http://content.time.com/time/subscriber/article/0,33009,723060,00.html.
6. Barbara Brown Taylor, "Bread of Angels," in *Bread of Angels* (Lanham, MD: Rowman & Littlefield, 1997), 10–11.
7. For more about the exhibit, see Nora McGreevy, "How an Art Exhibition in Breonna Taylor's Hometown Honors Her Life and Impact," *Smithsonian Magazine*, April 14, 2021, https://www.smithsonianmag.com/smart-news/louisville-exhibition-honors-breonna-taylor-180977503/.
8. Nap Ministry, https://thenapministry.wordpress.com. Tricia Hersey has now published a book titled *Rest Is Resistance: A Manifesto* (New York: Little, Brown Spark, 2022).
9. Gray Chapman, "The Atlanta Nap Ministry Preaches the Liberating Power of Rest," *Atlanta*, April 29, 2019, https://www.atlantamagazine.com/health/the-atlanta-nap-ministry-preaches-the-liberating-power-of-rest/.
10. Chapman, "Atlanta Nap Ministry."
11. Chapman, "Atlanta Nap Ministry."
12. Walter Brueggemann, "The Liturgy of Abundance, the Myth of Scarcity," *Christian Century*, March 24, 1999, https://www.christiancentury.org/article/2012-01/liturgy-abundance-myth-scarcity.
13. Wayne Muller, *Sabbath: Finding Rest, Renewal, and Delight in Our Busy Lives* (New York: Bantam Books, 1999), 1.
14. Muller, *Sabbath*, 3.
15. Muller, *Sabbath*, 3.
16. Cole Arthur Riley, *This Here Flesh: Spirituality, Liberation, and the Stories That Make Us* (New York: Convergent, 2022), 151.
17. Sonya Renee Taylor, post on her social media account, @sonyareneetaylor, April 2, 2020.

18. Richard Rohr, *Everything Belongs: The Gift of Contemplative Prayer* (New York: Crossroad Publishing, 2003), 62.

Palm Sunday and Holy Week

1. Willie Jennings and Miroslav Volf, "Joy and the Act of Resistance against Despair," *For the Life of the World*, Yale Center for Faith & Culture, February 28, 2021, https://for-the-life-of-the-world-yale-center-for-faith-culture.simplecast.com/episodes/joy-and-the-act-of-resistance-against-despair-willie-jennings-and-miroslav-volf-yUivB9ro.
2. Anathea Portier-Young, "Commentary on Exodus 17:1–7," Working Preacher, March 12, 2023, https://www.workingpreacher.org/preaching.aspx?commentary_id=3432.
3. Martin Luther King Jr., "The Other America" (speech at Stanford University, California, April 14, 1967). Transcript and video are available through the Civil Rights Movement Archive, https://www.crmvet.org/docs/otheram.htm.
4. Valerie Bridgeman, "Exodus 17:1–7," *First Reading* (podcast), September 27, 2020, https://firstreadingpodcast.com/podcast/exodus-171-7-with-valerie-bridgeman/.
5. Emily Freeman, *The Next Right Thing: A Simple, Soulful Practice for Making Life Decisions* (Grand Rapids: Revell, 2019), 15.
6. Martin Luther King Jr., *Stride toward Freedom: The Montgomery Story* (New York: Harper & Row, 1958), 134–35.
7. James Waddell Alexander, trans., "O Sacred Head, Now Wounded," in *Glory to God* (Louisville, KY: Westminster John Knox Press, 2013), #221.
8. Charles Wesley, "Love's Redeeming Work Is Done," in *Singing the Living Translation* (Boston: Unitarian Universalist Assoc., 1993), #268.
9. Shane Claiborne, *The Irresistible Revolution: Living as an Ordinary Radical* (Grand Rapids: Zondervan, 2006), 77–78.
10. Fred Craddock, *Luke*, Interpretation (Louisville, KY: Westminster John Knox Press, 1990), 278.

Printed in the USA
CPSIA information can be obtained
at www.ICGtesting.com
LVHW040614020224
770686LV00001B/27

9 780664 268176